*The Human Side
of M&A*

The Human Side of M&A

*Leveraging
the Most Important Factor
in Deal Making*

DENNIS C. CAREY

DAYTON OGDEN

with JUDITH A. ROLAND

OXFORD
UNIVERSITY PRESS
2004

OXFORD
UNIVERSITY PRESS

Oxford New York
Auckland Bangkok Buenos Aires Cape Town Chennai
Dar es Salaam Delhi Hong Kong Istanbul Karachi Kolkata
Kuala Lumpur Madrid Melbourne Mexico City Mumbai Nairobi
São Paulo Shanghai Taipei Tokyo Toronto

Copyright © 2004 by Oxford University Press, Inc.

Published by Oxford University Press, Inc.
198 Madison Avenue, New York, New York 10016
www.oup.com

Oxford is a registered trademark of Oxford University Press

Library of Congress Cataloging-in-Publication Data

Carey, Dennis C.
The human side of M&A : how CEOs leverage the most important asset in
deal making / Dennis C. Carey and Dayton Ogden.
    p. cm.
Includes bibliographical references and index.
ISBN 0-19-514096-6
1. Consolidation and merger of corporations.
2. Human capital.
3. Organizational effectiveness.
I. Ogden, Dayton.
II. Title.
HD2746.5 .C347 2004
658.3—dc22   2003026351

Book design by Adam B. Bohannon

9 8 7 6 5 4 3 2 1

Printed in the United States of America
on acid-free paper

With gratitude to my daughter, Maggie,
and my son, Matt,
whose patience and understanding
enabled me to complete this book
—Dennis C. Carey
October 30, 2003

To my incredibly patient and persevering wife, Peggy
—Dayton Ogden
October 30, 2003

CONTENTS

■

While we may never again match the volume of M&A activity of 1999—when the number of merger announcements reached an all-time high—M&A will continue to be a logical, efficient, and profitable strategy for many companies in a global economy. There are several sound bases for deciding to pursue this strategy, which we discuss in detail in the chapters that follow, and once a company decides to go this route, it must do everything possible to better its chances of success. Mistakes are not only expensive but also increasingly are carefully scrutinized by shareholders and the media as well as disruptive to a company's people and operations.

You will be building your merger or acquisition on a shaky foundation unless a few critical elements pass muster before the transaction is finalized. Specifically, you will need to ensure that:

1. **The strategy is sound.** Whether the goal is expanding markets, products, or consolidation, make sure that M&A is the right solution;
2. **There are no skeletons in the closet.** Make certain that you are not inheriting any fraud, legal, or accounting issues that could spell disaster for any deal. Be diligent about due diligence; and
3. **The human capital picture is thoroughly understood.** It is critical to follow a separate process that will uncover precisely what you will be getting in your new management team, a picture that will not be fleshed out sufficiently as a result of the normal due diligence process that focuses on financial and legal issues.

This book will concentrate on the third category in this list, the human capital element, encompassing such key themes as assessing the quality of the team; the necessity and potential of retraining; unifying the culture; and embracing the most effective compensation model. While we do not claim to be experts in every one of the topics that we cover in the book, we have had access to leading consultants as well as high-profile CEOs and directors who share their extensive and instructive experience in many of these areas. Categories 1 and 2—strategy and conventional due diligence—above are left to the many consultants specializing in these areas.

We find it remarkable how few companies truly understand the culture they are "buying" when they acquire or merge with another company. This factor, we firmly believe, is a primary cause of the many failures in the M&A arena. Greater understanding is the key to success. Armed with this knowledge companies can make informed and timely judgments, whether the decision is ultimately to walk away from an inappropriate deal or find ways to ameliorate differences that will sabotage efforts at meshing cultures and achieve the vision of the merger.

Regardless of high price tags, these transactions are often done in haste with a strategy consultant and without the required know-how to assess the people and to get a clear window into the organization. Those leading these deals frequently rely only on publicly available information, which is simply not adequate to form a proper knowledge base and may gloss over potential pitfalls.

The history of business is now replete with deals that held great promise but ultimately fell apart, often not long after the ink on the announcement was dry. There are many reasons why this can happen. Perhaps retention had not been carefully thought through and planned for. Up and comers who may have been one heartbeat away from the top were three or four heartbeats away after a merger. Often it is the compensation system that trips up the merger—a system that is not aligned and brought into synch with the merger's strategy and objectives. In pulling the trigger on the merger, handcuffs on the most desirable and hard to replace talent may be lost.

The bad news is that all of these scenarios, and others, can quickly let the air out of the merger balloon. But the good news is, with careful thought and planning, many of these missteps can be avoided.

That is what this book is all about. While not all pitfalls in the human capital domain can be sidestepped, many can. We believe that by following the guidelines recommended in this book, companies will achieve a higher rate of success when committing themselves, their employees, and their shareholders to mergers and acquisitions. Importantly, the advice we offer is practically based, from the viewpoint of insiders who have been there before those who may now be contemplating or planning these deals. They understand what works and doesn't work, and share their experiences from both ends of that spectrum.

Despite the yo-yo activity of M&A, which has its ups and downs in concurrence with a host of economic factors, M&A is not likely to go out of vogue and will surely continue to figure prominently in the strategy of many companies. Rightfully so. Carefully chosen as a course of action, and carefully planned for and monitored, it will continue to be a productive course to follow. We believe that the principles and recommendations we set forth in the following pages will serve those who follow this course well and will, we sincerely hope, enable them to learn from the experiences of others.

*The Human Side
of M&A*

CHAPTER I

Introduction

Improve the Odds

■

Knowledge is power.

Sir Francis Bacon, 1597

There was a great deal of excitement, both inside and outside the two organizations, when pharmaceutical company American Home Products and biotechnology company Monsanto announced merger plans on June 1, 1998. After all, American Home offered a formidable marketing infrastructure, with a sales force of 10,000, to launch products emerging from Monsanto's promising drug pipeline. Monsanto brought R&D expertise and an aggressive growth strategy, which American Home's financial resources could support. The two companies anticipated saving $1.5 billion over three years by closing redundant facilities and halting redundant R&D efforts. But less than five months later, merger plans had been scrapped.

It all sounded great. So why did things come to a screeching halt? In short, the two companies' cultures were completely mismatched, a fact that wasn't apparent from the start. As one pharmaceutical analyst put it, the merger was fraught with "incompatibilities at the top." A merger between a frugal, rigidly run company like American Home and a high-spending, risk-taking company like Monsanto was not an easy fit. For starters, decision makers from both sides couldn't even agree on who would run the combined company—or how. There were disagreements on issues across the board. What would be the proportion of funding for pharmaceutical versus ag-biotech products? What about the extent of projected lay-offs, and which company would make the bigger sacrifice? Who should be assigned to corporate headquarters?

In retrospect, it's easy to see why merger plans were abandoned, but unfortunately the two companies paid a substantial price for announcing the merger before it had been sufficiently vetted for potential problems. While the original merger announcement hardly sent a ripple through the markets, when the deal was called off on October 13, 1999, shareholders in both companies took a big hit. Monsanto shares dropped 27 percent (from $50.38 to $37), and American Home shares dropped 10 percent (from $50 to $44.88). And the case of American Home Products and Monsanto is not an anomaly.

There are steps companies can take before a merger is announced, and indeed at each step of the merger process, to improve their chances for success and, consequently, enhance the prospects for shareholders. That is the subject we tackle in this book, with a particular emphasis on human capital-related issues, since that is the sphere in which we operate.

Risky Business

Mergers and takeovers—even those of the mega variety—have become commonplace events. Nothing is considered too large or too ambitious. During 1999 there were more than 8,000 merger announcements—an all-time high—in the United States alone. The dollar value of the announced merger transactions involving U.S. targets during 1980–2002 was over $12 trillion.*

Although the pace of merger activity has slowed significantly from its peak in 1999, these corporate combinations will continue to figure importantly in the strategy of many companies. Fueled by a number of factors—including globalization, which has vastly expanded the scope of traditional markets; deregulation of industries; technological advances that have opened the door to new cross-industry partnerships; and a competitive climate that has forced companies to become both more efficient and more creative—M&A will continue to be a path of choice for many companies in the years ahead.

Looking back at a history of mergers and acquisitions, it is clear that not all of these deals are successful; indeed, both the successes and failures have been fairly well chronicled in the press and in management literature. By some estimates about two-thirds of deals that are publicly announced will ultimately either fail to take place or will fail to produce anywhere near the shareholder value anticipated. As always, the old saw "the bigger they come the harder they fall" seems to prove true. Some of the larger mergers have been staggering disappointments to shareholders, either falling apart over unforeseen culture issues or by demonstrating once again that bigger is not necessarily better. The merger of AOL Time Warner, which was announced with great excitement about the "synergy" between new technology and classic content, proved to disappoint on all counts.

* This information, taken from our original research, forms the methodological foundation of this book. For our complete analysis of the largest mergers that have subsequently produced the greatest shareholder wealth, please refer to our complete report in the Appendix, at the back of this book.

Why are so few mergers successful? While we are wary of generalizing, it's safe to say that many who enter into these transactions are focused on the prize and are not equipped with the information they need to succeed and avoid pitfalls. As the pace of M&A activity has multiplied, so too has the knowledge and the level of required expertise. Mergers that may once have been merely a matter of financial accounting and due diligence now frequently give rise to a host of issues requiring broad consultation. Legal and regulatory matters, compensation and personnel questions, integration and leadership strategies, along with complex financial and accounting questions, are now a routine part of every significant deal. As a result, the demand for information about every aspect of M&A transactions has escalated.

The supply of practical information, however, has not kept pace with demand. Despite the abundance of published material on mergers, the world of merger strategy and tactics remains highly secretive. Because every acquisition plan involves market-sensitive information, chief executives are reluctant to discuss thoughts about possible deals or elaborate on problems with recently consummated mergers. There are few opportunities open to CEOs eager to exchange views with other corporate leaders who may be more experienced and knowledgeable about the mechanics and strategy of mergers.

That is why we decided to write this book: to help fill the information vacuum. Armed with the knowledge they need in key areas related to M&A, CEOs and directors will be in a more enlightened and confident position to decide whether to pursue plans in the first place and, later, assuming the merger has been consummated, to ensure that the pairing will achieve anticipated results.

Powerful Forces

Before examining the variables that influence the ultimate rise or fall of mergers, let's consider some of the powerful, unrelenting forces that are driving the merger phenomenon. And it is indeed a new phenomenon. Although the concept of a merger is as old as business itself, the pace, size, and scope of recent mergers have created a new and not so rare species—one that would have been unimaginable previously.

Why this rapid shift in scale? Once only a few industries were dominated by two or three "super titans": running shoes (Reebok, Nike, and Adidas); breakfast cereal (Kellogg's, General Mills, and Post); and hamburgers (Wendy's, McDonald's, and Burger King) are well-known examples. But the massive business consolidation that has taken place in one industry after another suggests that giants like these will increasingly emerge from once fragmented industries as diverse as financial services, pharmaceuticals, and oil and gas. Indeed, this trend seems to be occurring across the board. It would be difficult to overstate the level of change that consolidations on this plane bring with them as part of the package. In this active M&A environment, every company—whether or not it is currently contemplating a merger strategy—should consider the implications of a merger or takeover.

The factors driving the high level of mergers and acquisitions activity are many and varied. Deregulation is toppling governmental barriers, while the globalization of business is rendering geographic obstacles meaningless. Market volatility is creating new buying opportunities, particularly in Asia, while at the same time producing paper profits to be utilized by potential purchasers.

Deflation has made it difficult for once highly profitable

industries such as oil and gas to rethink their strategies. The alliance of Mobil and Exxon, for example, was driven in part by the impact of deflation and the difficulty of going it alone in such an environment. Deflation has also made it easier to afford takeovers, while access to large amounts of capital at relatively low rates is making it easier to finance them.

New accounting rules are providing fresh incentives to merge. Favorable tax and trade environments that facilitate cross-border trading within multinational corporations are adding to the advantages of global mergers. Finally, every company faces pressure to do what the competition is doing.

Higher Stakes Now

While the volume of M&A transactions has fallen off since its peak a few years ago, the aggregate of these deals has always been cyclical. Since companies can often gain great advantage in the marketplace through a merger or acquisition, there is little doubt activity will once again pick up. Certainly the M&A boom from the mid-1990s until 2001 was unprecedented among other peaks in the cycle—some five times greater than any previous ones.

Given a somewhat turbulent economy, there may be another wave in the making. In the October 14, 2002, issue of *Business Week* it was noted that "CEOs are compulsive dealmakers. Indeed, after a brief lull, their appetites will likely quicken when they see prices of other companies falling faster than their own. About 5,400 deals worth $346 billion were announced through September 30 (2002), according to Mergerstat. Even though that's way behind 1999's record $1.4 trillion, it could match the 1996 score of $470 billion."

Business Week's analysis asserts that, while the volume of deals will likely pick up yet again, the deal-making skills of CEOs and the ultimate success of these combinations have not improved. Although the price of failure has always been a severe burden to companies and their shareholders, the stakes are even higher now. "The price of failure is rising sharply. Until this year, companies could bury their bad deals on their balance sheets as goodwill—basically the difference between what they paid and the value of the assets that they acquired. Goodwill was quietly expensed over a period as long as 40 years. No longer. As AOL Time Warner, Inc. shareholders are painfully aware, companies now have to take a write-off straight away if the assets deteriorate in value."

New SEC regulations mean that potential mergers will be scrutinized much more carefully, leading to deal making that is trickier than ever. New accounting regulations will require companies to provide more in-depth information on proposed acquisitions, including details on all the advantages that will accrue to them as a result of the transaction.

Mergers get derailed, according to the *Business Week* study, when "companies dither over integrating operations after the merger, frustrating customers and employees and delaying capturing potential benefits." We could not agree more, and it is precisely this terrain, which can be tough to navigate, that we cover in this book. Without careful integration, the most promising deal will quickly fall apart.

Learning from Leaders

Throughout the course of this book, we provide insights from CEOs and consultants who have experienced success in the art and science of M&A transactions. Some of these individuals have been drawn from our research and head some of the most highly respected companies operating today. Other insights come from our experience consulting with clients involved in various stages of the M&A process, from initial management evaluation of a target to post-deal integration.

In the course of our work we have learned that regardless of the company or industry, M&A carries significant risks. Delineating and pursuing a strategy is only one critical part of the entire process. Most mergers—even those that are ultimately less successful—sounded good on paper: There were solid business reasons for going forward with them; the numbers added up; they passed due diligence and were most often recommended by investment bankers and strategy consultants.

Yet in many cases, the highly variable human element—the softer side of the deal that is not as obvious or as easy to quantify—was not accounted for. These cultural issues that we have learned are so crucial to the longer-term success of mergers need to be sifted through and assessed, and judgments made as to the likelihood of success of any corporate union. If a decision is made to proceed after all the financial and human capital issues are assessed, companies must anticipate the cultural roadblocks they will confront when the companies merge and how they will deal with them.

Fortunately many potential problems can be foreseen, and a number of companies with a track record in successful M&A transactions are willing to share their experiences on what has and has not worked for them. These experiences, and our own observations based on our work with many of these companies, form the foundation of this book. In looking to these leaders in M&A, we reckoned, why not learn from the best of the best, not only practices that are recommended but also those to avoid?

Our Perspective

We would like to state at the outset that we are not financial consultants. Indeed, there is a well-occupied niche of professionals advising on the financial side of M&A. Our expertise is on the human side of a complex equation, which with a great deal of research, advance planning, and luck may add up to a worthwhile deal. We both have a long and extensive track record working with CEOs and boards of directors to find the best talent. We do not offer guidance on the potential strategic fit between two merging companies. We assume that this has already been done and that all parties are satisfied that the combined organization will provide clear strategic advantages.

In 1995 we founded a separate Spencer Stuart business called Global Intelligence, later renamed Strategic Leadership Services, which specializes evaluating talent and organizational culture relative to succession planning, premerger and acquisition due diligence, postmerger and acquisition integration, and industry benchmarking. Given the ongoing and direct exposure we've had counseling CEOs involved in various phases of M&A transactions, it's hardly surprising that we've developed some very strong opinions about what human factors correlate with success and failure in this arena. Thus this book.

In attempting to assess success or failure and quantify it in some way, it is only natural to look for patterns. Why does one organization succeed where another fails? In a process that calls for a vast commitment in terms of resources—financial as well as human—how can we learn from the experience of others? This approach, of codifying and emulating the best practices of those who have achieved the most impressive results and sidestepped apparent pitfalls, is one we advocated in our first book, *CEO Succession*, and one we adhere to again in this book, just as we practice it every day in our work with clients.

While drawing liberally from our own experience and from CEOs we know well, we also wanted to balance our personal point of view with a rigorous analysis by a qualified statistician of the most successful mergers that have been accomplished in the past ten years.

We enlisted the cooperation of Dr. Sanjai Bhagat, a well-known and respected corporate governance expert and professor of finance at the University of Colorado's School of Business. Dr. Bhagat's research comprises the appendix at the end of this book and provides readers with a broader framework in which to consider our views and those of the individuals we interviewed.

A Reader's Roadmap

We have organized the book in a generally chronological fashion, based on key human-related issues companies are likely to confront in the course of a merger.

In this first chapter, "Improve the Odds," we lay the foundation for the succeeding chapters. The volume and overall growth of M&A deals may hardly be news to the reader, but the lack of fulfillment of the promise of many of them may come as a surprise.

Our thesis, which is reinforced throughout the book, is that scrutinizing the financial side of these transactions is only half of the equation, and it is hardly an assurance of success. In the chapters that follow we leave the financial scrutiny to the many capable consultants already covering this territory as we explore the human capital side of the equation. Awareness of the potential culture conflicts and other people-related issues is important to ward off mergers that will fall short of their promise. Also important is learning to recognize which problems should put a nix on a deal under consideration as well as knowing what can be done to ameliorate any problems that can be managed.

In chapter 2, "Take Stock of Human Capital," we step back before a merger occurs. While a company is still contemplating whether or not to proceed—and before any official announcement—there should be a thorough assessment of the functional skills each party brings to the table. At a minimum, any executive contemplating a merger should know the answers to a series of questions that can determine how well the merged company will ultimately operate: What are the skills and leadership potential of the target company? How do they stack up against the competition? How will this team handle the stress of the merger and postmerger challenges? There should also be a careful consideration of the blending of human capital assets, and all of these issues must be carefully thought out before you pull the trigger.

In chapter 3, "Create a New Vision," we discuss why it is advisable to have a thorough evaluation of management teams and prevailing cultures before, during, and after a merger. It will be important to identify players in the companies who are wedded to the old way of doing things and would likely be roadblocks to the creation of a new vision and a new culture. Before the merger, such an evaluation can give a seal of approval to a particular deal or, conversely, rule out a combination that could be a prescription for disaster. Assuming there is a green light to proceed, during and after the merger, the results of such an audit can assist in the synthesis of the two organizations, ensure that key players are in the right place, and generally help smooth the way for the merger to fulfill its promise.

The period between the merger announcement and regulatory approval, which we turn our attention to in chapter 4, "Retain and Motivate Key Players," can be a difficult one to navigate. There is an information vacuum as companies are under regulatory and legal constraints about sharing information. Yet there is often a palpable level of anxiety among employees concerning their roles, and long-term survival, in the about-to-be reconfigured organization. Headhunters, smelling blood, dangle opportunities before employees who are uncertain about their future. We discuss some compensation and benefits strategies that can provide reassurance and stability during this period.

The early key decisions that must be made concerning the structure of the new entity are the subject of chapter 5, "Integrate Deliberately and Swiftly." Move quickly once a merger is a go, most executives told us. Despite some of the dangers inherent in pushing ahead before a deal gets its final approval, most leaders are willing to assume some risk in the interest of getting the enterprise up and going as soon as possible. Many underscored the critical importance of hitting the ground running on the first official day of operating as a combined company. In this chapter, we discuss some of the key elements of integration from the point of view of those who have been through it, as well as how to avoid some of the dangers inherent in the process and how to minimize risk.

Once the two companies have agreed to merge but may still be awaiting regulatory approval, as we discuss in chapter 6, "Survive the Regulatory Process," a particularly difficult period of limbo may set in. Integration must be under way during this period but must be undertaken with great care when the outcome of the deal is not 100 percent certain. One cautionary tale and some guidelines from survivors and former regulators help those facing regulatory hurdles.

We examine some critical issues in chapter 7, "Beef Up the Board." Who survives on the board? Indeed, what should the board of the new entity look like? While it can be difficult to recruit directors after a merger—and there is certainly a general lack of CEO candidates available to serve—the good news is there is a real chance to diversify the board by identifying specific skills and experience required and recruiting directors who fill these gaps. M&A can provide a one-time opportunity to put some best governance practices into action, including a leaner board and one that better represents the interests of shareholders. Because good directors are increasingly hard to find, don't overlook capable directors on the boards of acquisitions. They can prove to be excellent resources who may also be able to provide the required institutional memory and continuity.

As consultants on the human capital side of mergers, in chapter 8, we synthesize our final thoughts and advice with those of acquirers we have interviewed for the book. We summarize our top-line thinking on how companies, with thoughtful, careful planning, can improve their chances of success in M&A and lessen the likelihood that they will become another statistic on the lengthy and growing list of failed corporate marriages.

In the appendix, "Smart Money and Smart Bidders," we provide insight into the methodological underpinnings for the book. Dr. Sanjai Bhagat, a professor of finance at the University of Colorado at Boulder, shares the details of his in-depth analysis of the biggest successful M&A deals (determined by increase in shareholder value) of the past ten years. We have not confined ourselves to the list that emerged from this analysis. Indeed, there is a lot to learn from companies that may not be in the pantheon of the most successful mergers and acquisitions. But the list was an important jumping-off point and a critical benchmark throughout our work on the book.

Francis Bacon's celebrated aphorism, "Knowledge is power," is as relevant and apt—both as a statement and an admonition—today as it was more than four hundred years ago. Clearly the companies that truly do their homework, or due diligence, in testing the numbers and examining the human components that comprise a deal, stand a far better chance of reaping the desired benefits of a merger or acquisition than those that do not. In this book, we share with our readers a process for gaining that all-important intelligence and putting it to work. We are confident that greater attention to the human side of these deals, combined with the proper tools to evaluate and integrate management teams, will help ensure far greater chances of success. We sincerely hope that the information we provide contributes to an intelligent, well-thought-out M&A process and consequently greater success for companies that choose this strategic path.

CHAPTER 2

Take Stock of Human Capital

■

Leadership assessment is really indispensable in M&A. Very often, particularly when you're talking about an acquisition, not a merger of equals, the assumption is that no one from the acquired company will be an asset to the business, but that just doesn't make sense. You're not just acquiring products. If you have good products, you must have good people who developed and market them.

Daniel J. Phelan, senior vice president
of human resources for Glaxo SmithKline

Properly evaluating the human side of the merger or acquisition and getting the management team in place is critical to the success of these transactions. Setting up and evaluating a human balance sheet is a tricky proposition, but that is what we recommend companies do when contemplating a merger. At the outset of merger discussions, at least a preliminary investigation of how management teams will fit together—including strengths, weaknesses, and gaps—is important. After that initial phase, if and when discussions become more serious, the human capital assessment must become more rigorous as well.

A human capital audit is a complicated process with many variables. When dealing with numbers, no matter how complicated the formula, one ultimately arrives at an answer. And, given the implementation of a disciplined process, others should be able to arrive at more or less the same conclusion.

Not so when evaluating people. Humans are complex beings, each with his or her unique personality, faults, behavior, likes, and dislikes. Getting beneath the surface and accounting for all of the factors that may be relevant to the success or failure of a reassembled management team is not an easy task, though it is essential to get an accurate reading while still in the due diligence phase of a merger.

The fact that this is a difficult task, however, does not mean it cannot be accomplished. In fact, we perform these sorts of human capital analyses all the time in our Strategic Leadership Services practice. Usually they help confirm that a merger that looks promising on paper has the management wherewithal to achieve desired objectives. Occasionally the analysis raises red flags that may lead to an acquirer changing its mind about proceeding with a specific deal. Either way, it is best for there to be as many knowns as possible before proceeding or retrenching, and companies have the added comfort of knowing that their decision was made with the assistance of solid research.

The key challenge for the merging organizations is to take stock of a full menu of human capital issues quickly. The added wrinkle is that this must be done in a period when there may be regulatory delays and frequently rampant uncertainty. On the one hand you're making absolutely crucial decisions about the human side of the house when you don't even know if you will be allowed to go forward. The stress produced by the uncertainty is hard to overstate.

The underlying premises in this chapter are that the best way to cope with this uncertainty and stress is to:

- Have an experienced, objective third party advise and help assess human capital

- Implement and rely on a superb, transparent process for dealing with a range of dicey related issues
- Optimize internal communications to defuse the inevitable insecurity, anxiety, and stress

In this chapter we discuss specific guidelines on systematically collecting the information that is critical to possess before going beyond the phase of mere casual interest in a merger.

Accounting for the Human Element

The world's best strategy and projections mean little if a company does not possess a management team capable of carrying out well-laid plans. When determining if, how, and when to proceed with a particular deal, perhaps the most important consideration in the calculus has to do with people. People are always complex and a merger magnifies those complexities in many overt and subtle ways.

Geometrically compounding the complexities represented by the human assets is the culture of the two organizations that are coming together. Behavior of individual executives is conditioned not only by their own particular management, but also by the cumulative influences that the culture of their organization rewards and penalizes. Accordingly, it is absolutely crucial in premerger circumstances to gain as much useful information as possible about the human assets on the other side. This information will be used as a basis for the seal of approval to go ahead with the deal or, conversely, to nix it altogether.

There is no foolproof method for conducting meaningful

and valuable human capital evaluations, but there are time-tested techniques for assessing key people and predicting how they are likely to perform and behave in a combined organization. These assessment and predictive techniques are similar to those used by sophisticated executive recruiters conducting high-level executive searches. There is nothing particularly mysterious about the process, and you don't have to have been trained by the CIA in order to pull it off. In-depth, targeted reference checking and the publicly available record about what has been accomplished by an executive in both key functional and general management roles can help to flesh out a picture of an individual's strengths and weaknesses in a particular corporate setting.

Data collected from public and private outlets serve as testaments to soft issues, such as management style, listening skills, sense of humor, and leadership force, as well as harder issues, such as specific business results, financial performance, new strategic initiatives, product launches, financial management skills, and relationships with the Street. Assembling these pieces of the puzzle and combining them with a little extrapolation produces a fairly complete and accurate portrait of an individual. And we have found that past performance—whether successful or not—is highly predictive of future performance.

The public record, particularly now with ready access to the web, is something virtually anyone can obtain. With this information it is quite simple to determine the impact an individual executive had as, say, the head of a division, by examining the performance of that division under his or her tenure. If you're willing to research the public record and then test, with knowledgeable third-party sources, the role a specific individual has played in creating good, mediocre, or poor results, you can get a good handle on performance issues. Throughout this process it is critical to triangulate. By considering multiple sources you inoculate against dealing merely with one person's set of biases. Inevitably, after the research is supplemented by keen reference checking by a pro who knows how to unearth critical information, a pattern regarding an individual's personality, his or her career moves, and history each step of the way will take shape. And the premise that a person's history portends his or her future, and that this information can be extracted and assembled into a very telling picture with the application of an analytical tool kit, is the underlying basis for our Strategic Leadership Services practice.

Operating within Constraints

Through Strategic Leadership Services we try to make highly informed predictions about executives' behavior as well as highly educated guesses about the contribution they will likely make to the success of the anticipated combined organization. These judgments are not nearly as much of a leap as they might sound to someone unfamiliar with the process. By assessing all of the varied sources of information we have already mentioned—the public record on past and current accomplishments and knowledgeable third-party sources, including former colleagues, to assess work style and temperament—we can put together a detailed picture of an individual.

Taking stock of human assets should begin ideally in the due diligence phase and can effectively be done through the application of some form of intelligence gathering. During this phase, any assessment must be conducted on a very discreet basis, because the deal hasn't yet been publically disclosed.

When the organizations have pulled the trigger and have agreed to merge, in many cases they are in that awful no-man's-land that exists pending regulatory approval. This period may range from several months to one or more years, and there are certain prohibitions on what companies in these circumstances are allowed to do. If there are, for example, two telecommunications organizations, it's fine to say in theory, "Let's have a transition team integrate those two wireless divisions and decide what their strategy is going to be." But, until the regulatory authorities give the green light for the merger to go forward, there are huge risks associated with having the management teams from the two companies sit down and hammer out a strategy. The risks include:

- Disclosure of important confidential information
- Demotivation of key executives who perceive they're going to be losers
- Potential paralysis of the previous strategies that were driving those businesses when they were separate
- Clash between people and culture, creating an unhealthy climate for change

Communicating and planning—and, particularly, sharing confidential information such as strategy—presents a significant threat at this stage.

Outside Expertise

Given regulatory and other constraints immediately after a merger, certain tasks must be accomplished, and some cannot practically be done by anyone on either company's management team or even a combined transition team. The transition team comprises people who possess their own biases, ambitions, and insecurities. Entrusted with responsibility that potentially creates huge conflicts of interest, transition teams desperately need objective outside advice in order to minimize the inevitable politics and conflicts that these responsibilities represent.

In any merger or acquisition, both sides need strategic advice that at least sets out for the top management and CEOs the new overarching vision for the combined companies. That is not necessarily a full strategy review. The vision elaborates on the precise reasons for doing the deal and spells out what synergies are going to be attempted right from the start to begin to achieve those goals. In the case of Citigroup and Travelers, for example, the vision would have been cross-selling, building a world-class wholesale bank to complement the retail franchise.

The second area in which both management teams need assistance is in defining what kind of people they will need to have in place to fulfill the vision. What are the specs for key executive jobs that will help to propel the vision? What are the specs for other critical roles?

After the specs are developed, companies in the throes of a merger need advice regarding which people in the combined organization best fit those criteria. They need to know which members of the current management team are most critical to retain and therefore require individual "handcuffs" and special attention during the period of uncertainty. They need a quick inventory of whom they are going to keep. The process goes beyond choosing who the best candidates are for the top jobs to identifying key people in other areas of the companies. In some companies, R&D, for example, might be critical to success in the market, and losing key players there can hurt the value of the enterprise. Quickly identifying and taking steps to retain key people in that part of the company would, then, be critical to the success of the merger.

At this stage, companies also need to know what the human capital implications will be for the technology strategy they settle on for the combined business. Will technology be driven centrally by a small group of development types who report to the top of the house, or is it going to be developed on a decentralized basis? It is hugely important to get your arms around this early. Technology executives are in great demand, and if you don't deal with these issues quickly, you may lose valuable talent that is virtually impossible to replace.

Another area that must be carefully attended to is compensation and benefits. Missteps here can quickly lead to damaging defections as well as lingering problems with remaining management. Nothing inhibits the potential success of a merger more than protracted delays in developing a unified approach to compensation and benefits. Questions arise immediately over the appropriate mix between fixed and variable compensation. What is the role of stock options? What are the appropriate policies for time not worked, sick leave, maternity leave, vacation, excused absences, and a variety of related issues? Each company has a unique culture, and finding a middle ground that will please everyone on sensitive issues such as compensation is exceedingly difficult.

In summary, the key challenge for the merging organizations is to take stock of a full menu of human capital issues quickly in a regulatory environment that makes it difficult in the face of delays, rampant uncertainty, and a high degree of anxiety at all levels. Our experience in this area has convinced us that the only way to cope with this uncertainty is to rely on the advice of a sophisticated, objective, and experienced third party, on the one hand, and to follow a process on the other hand. Companies that rely on the expertise of an objective third party that has been through the process before, and adhere to a good, reliable process for evaluation and decision making will be way ahead of the game. Following this route and complementing it with optimal internal communications, which can serve to defuse a great deal of the inevitable insecurity, anxiety, and stress, will lead to a far greater chance of success in the long run.

GTE's Experience

The GTE Bell Atlantic merger became effective on June 30, 2000, creating Verizon Communications, "a formidable new competitor in global communications," according to the company press release. The new company operated under the leadership of Charles R. Lee, Verizon chairman, and Ivan Seidenberg, Verizon president and CEO.

During the period after the announcement of the planned merger and prior to regulatory approval, GTE and Bell Atlantic underwent a rigorous strategic leadership assessment, as the two companies evaluated management's strengths vis-à-vis the anticipated combination. J. Randall MacDonald, currently senior vice president of human resources for IBM but then executive vice president of human resources for GTE, was involved in the entire process and helped guide it from beginning to end.

"When you think about two organizations coming together that are perhaps competitors, they likely don't understand the personality, behavior, and competencies that exist on the other side because of the adverse relationship. It makes a lot of sense to try to put some objectivity into a process of selection," says MacDonald, reflecting on the role the strategic leadership assessment played in the success of the merger. "So, the first advantage is that it allows for objectivity. Secondly, there is a lot of value in having the assessment done by people who do this for a living day in and day out and who must be professionally objective. They have experience with what the skill sets are, what criteria people should be judged against. This allows people within the respective organizations to have a comfort level: 'Gee, I'm actually talking to somebody who knows my discipline or knows my industry.' Moreover, from an M&A standpoint, it's helpful to get substantive examples of accomplishments as opposed to hearsay and to read consistent reports where everybody is being judged against the same competencies and criteria."

As good as MacDonald believed GTE's experience was with the strategic leadership process, he gives an unvarnished view that includes the minor negatives in a process he still views as very valuable. "The downside of this," says MacDonald, "is that everybody is looking exactly for that, the downside. And there will be a lot of questions and uncertainty: 'What's really going on here?' 'Did somebody really have an agenda?' 'Do they really understand the business?' People may assume that there is a built-in bias, that the cards are stacked in favor of the organization that brought in the third party to assist in assessments."

MacDonald adds that the process is costly and time-consuming, but believes that the pluses outweigh the minuses. It enables companies to gather a lot of valuable information about people on both management teams and makes the task of selecting and synthesizing a management team more rational and less political because there are objective analyses to back your decisions.

The strategic leadership assessment process helps uncover unintentional and unconscious bias, so that those trying to fashion one management team out of two separate entities obtain as complete an assessment of the players as possible.

There are always a few surprises—assessments of individuals that may not quite jibe with the way they may have been perceived by those at the top. "There is no doubt about it," says MacDonald, "we all have blind spots. You may assume that one manager is going to show better, only to be told something different by outside experts. In certain cases this did happen to us, particularly where someone may have been overlooked, and it gave us pause. It forced us to say, 'Hey what's going on here? Maybe there is something that we're not seeing,' which I think has real value. The entire process is confirming and reassuring."

Legal issues are always first and foremost when we work with clients on strategic leadership projects, and efforts to minimize legal exposure may be something we worry about more than they do. Clients will need to carefully consider how they use, and safeguard, the management intelligence we provide. Once companies have used the data to assist with crucial management integration decisions, individual evaluations often continue to be of use to human resources executives. The information helps to complete profiles of key executives and can be used as a development tool.

Achieving "Buy-in"

Assuming that a company decides that a Strategic Leadership Services process would provide valuable data to set priorities for integrating management teams and shaping a vision and strategy for the newly combined company, we have some recommendations on how best to proceed. Key to the ability to develop useful information and, ultimately, the key to the success of the entire project is achieving buy-in from management of the company that is being scrutinized. The assessment must be accomplished in a way that enables all parties to accept the validity of such an exercise.

When we launched the Strategic Leadership Services project with GTE for the merger with Bell Atlantic, there was some initial anxiety about what we were doing and what the information would be used for. In some cases, managers were somewhat threatened. But as things proceeded, executives were eager to be included in the assessments, and the process was pushed further and further down through the organization, quickly generating overall enthusiasm and buy-in.

Based on GTE's success with the process, Randy MacDonald has some advice for companies contemplating strategic leadership assessment: "Do it incrementally, let people get comfortable with it. They need to see how the process works, where it works, when it works, who it works for. They need to understand the why."

A merger in the making creates a high-anxiety environment, and everyone is nervous about change. This is actually a rational response and easy to understand: Suddenly their world has changed; they're not necessarily working for the company they thought they were working for. "They are working for a new entity and there are people on the other side of the aisle, the Democrats and the Republicans, so to speak, and they all have to come together and walk down the aisle together. That's uncomfortable. So, do it in small bites and start at the top as opposed to starting at the bottom," advises Mac-Donald.

There is an important psychological reason for starting at the top with this assessment, and it may have a significant impact on getting willing participants and the most reliable information. Starting the process at a lower level of management may make executives even more anxious and paranoid about their future. In this situation, the assessment may be perceived as an attempt to go after middle management rather than the rightful goal of the exercise: to achieve a balanced view of the entire array of management resources that will aid in integrating the two companies. Starting at the top helps convey the message that the process is valuable and enables the organization to get the buy-in required, at all levels.

Glaxo SmithKline: The Importance of Process

Companies that have achieved success in meshing cultures make it look like a systematic, easy process. More often than not, however, they are the exceptions. Integrating cultures isn't something that just happens fortuitously. It is the product of exhaustive planning and anticipation. When the task of merging cultures is approached carelessly or callously, results can be devastating, and the hopes and dreams of what the merger was to achieve can go out the window. A merger partner or acquisition target can easily fail to fulfill its promise if employees who may have been critical to success do not become part of the new entity. When this happens, it can be a little like killing the goose that laid the golden egg. The object—easier said than done—is to preserve whatever it was about the management team and the culture that made a company an attractive target to begin with, and then to fold that into the new entity.

It's not surprising that the strongest advocates of using a systematic leadership assessment process are companies that have been involved in mergers or acquisitions in which the combination has been less than optimal. Integration problems following a merger often lead companies to implement a more effective process the next time. This was certainly the case with the merger between Glaxo and SmithKline Beecham in 2000.

A veteran of previous mergers, Daniel J. Phelan, senior vice president of human resources for Glaxo SmithKline, declares, "After the process we have been through in other mergers, we would never get involved in a merger with another company without going through a formal assessment process."

"There were a number of important objectives we were able to achieve using this process," says Phelan. "First of all, it enabled us to get a better reading on people. From the viewpoint of employees, it leveled the playing field—all those involved felt they were getting a fair shake before we made decisions on who would finally get what job. And it was good for overall morale, which can often take a beating during a merger. Because it was a third party doing the evaluations, the process was perceived as more objective and people felt good about it.

"After we announced the merger," Phelan explains, "we knew we wanted to do a management assessment. The question was how far to go. Initially we thought it would entail only those people who reported directly to the executive team—top management."

The process began at the top, with the fourteen-member executive team for the merger: one-half from Glaxo Wellcome and one-half from SmithKline Beecham. Before going deeper into both organizations, an initial round of interviews provided a good sense of cultural differences and expectations of the merger and the selection process. After the first series of interviews was completed, Spencer Stuart presented the results to the top management of both companies.

Timing Can Be Tricky

Even when a merger seems likely to proceed and an assessment of the management team is expected to help guide the process, deciding when to embark on the process, and identifying key members of an executive team for the merged entity going forward, can be a complicated issue. It's a careful balance to strike. On the one hand, companies cannot go blithely ahead without any regard for the possibility that a deal may not be finalized; many do indeed fall apart, even at the last minute. On the other hand, there is a great deal of integration work to be done before the deal gets a seal of approval and companies can operate under one banner. Merged companies that have not done the prep work and are not ready to roll on opening day may be at a serious disadvantage.

So what should you do? If it looks like the merger is going to happen, sometimes the best thing to do is to keep your fingers crossed, roll up your sleeves, and determine a workable agenda for management assessment and integration of the new team.

Top management of soon-to-be-formed Glaxo SmithKline worried about the timing and sharing of competitive information with a not-yet-guaranteed partner, but decided to make a leap of faith that the deal would go through.

The proposed deal between Glaxo and SmithKline Beecham was announced on January 17, 2000, and the stock for the combined company traded for the first time on December 27, 2000. Top managers engineering the management integration didn't know exactly when the deal would be approved, which made their work difficult. "We thought it would close in September," said Phelan, "but it's hard to know when you should tell people they either have a job or they don't. Assuming a September deadline, we thought we should tell them in July. But it really is a delicate balance. You may get a curve ball that can delay the deal three or four months. So you're faced with a dilemma: If you don't move fast enough, you lose people; if you move too fast, you alienate them."

It would be difficult to overestimate the anxiety and tension gnawing at companies during this limbo period, and the longer employees remain in an information vacuum, the greater the negative repercussions for morale and productivity. Some planning must be done, methodically and swiftly, even with only a tentative schedule of how and when the merger will be finalized. Pros who have been through the process agree on one thing: Do your homework. If you wait until the merger is finalized to integrate, you will never catch up.

Matching the New Team with the New Strategy

Assessments of individual managers during a merger require a great deal of knowledge about a new entity—the combined organization. A thorough understanding of the strategy of the new company that does not yet exist and the type of managers and competencies that will be required to propel it are essential.

How were priorities set for whom to evaluate? With two organizations and literally thousands of individuals, where does it make sense to begin, and where is the cutoff for management assessments? The assessment process with Smith-Kline and Glaxo Wellcome began with the top managers of each company. In essence, our initial task was to determine who would be critical to retain, or those managers whose loss would likely prove detrimental to the goals of the combined company.

Those put through the assessment process included direct reports to both executive teams and three to four levels down in R&D, where identifying and retaining talent was particularly critical. The total number assessed was about twice the number the companies originally anticipated evaluating. "In the end, we left the process open," explained Phelan. "If executives in a particular area wanted to continue the process further down, they had that option. For my staff, we used the process to select my eight direct reports. We referenced and interviewed candidates from both companies. The process was so successful, we decided to use the same criteria when we did our own evaluations later on."

In all, Spencer Stuart assessed some 400 people for about 160 jobs, in interviews that lasted from about one and a half to two hours. People had the opportunity to talk about themselves and what made them candidates for particular positions in the combined company. The process was highly individualized and managers were given a lot of time to talk.

One of the reasons assessments are welcomed by those being evaluated and provide valuable data to those assembling a management team is that participants view them as more of a hearing than an assessment, with the same ground rules applying to everyone. In the pressured environment surrounding a merger, people often find it a relief to talk about themselves and about where they may view themselves in the new company. They feel they are moving a step closer to some resolution of their own future.

It is important to remember that the interviews are one part of the overall assessment mix that helps determine the face of the new management team for the combined company. "Spencer Stuart was not making the actual decisions," said Phelan. "The information they provided was one piece of data to be considered, along with the data from the two separate organizations."

When looking to create one management team out of two,

decision makers should make an effort to get a balance of people from both companies. Ultimately, however, the goal is to retain the best people from both organizations, so balance for political reasons must come second.

How often, we wondered, were the data we provided from our assessments critical to making required management decisions? "In more cases than not," Phelan informed us, "it was used as a tie breaker." When the results of the interviews were shared with Phelan and SmithKline Beecham's CEO, Jean-Pierre Garnier, and Glaxo Wellcome's chairman, Sir Richard Sykes, the reaction, according to Phelan, was, "How could they do such a great job evaluating this person to this degree in an hour and a half? There were no cases where the reaction was 'this is so far off.' The accuracy amazed us."

AT&T: Focused on the Numbers

Some companies seem determined to learn from past mistakes; others seem destined to repeat them. Daniel Phelan indicated that Glaxo SmithKline would never consider another merger where the upfront homework on culture and assessing and combining management teams was not done to perfection. But even with billions of dollars at stake, some companies repeat a less-than-successful approach to the initial assessment of a potential merger and to postmerger integration.

AT&T is a good example of a company that, according to some insiders, appeared to be blind to a number of merger-related booby traps and consequently continued to repeat history rather than learn from it. Recently retired longtime AT&T executive vice president of human resources Hal Burlingame, who is now senior executive adviser to AT&T Wireless (a fully independent company that spun off from

AT&T in 2001), has a broad and deep perspective on AT&T and the many mergers it has been involved in over the years. Merger activity became particularly intense after C. Michael Armstrong took over as CEO in 1997. Armstrong had been CEO of Hughes Electronics Corporation since 1993, and had been responsible for the launch of DIRECTV, Hughes's direct-to-home digital broadcast business, and prior to that had spent thirty-one years at IBM, where he rose through the ranks from systems engineer to become senior vice president and chairman of the board of IBM World Trade Corporation.

AT&T's series of deals took its toll on the company, primarily, it seems, because of the focus on numbers, often to the exclusion of addressing key cultural factors, or impediments, between the organizations that would impact anticipated synergies. In addition, the board appeared to provide an inadequate counterbalance to a CEO seemingly more intent on making deals than on making them work.

The seeds of many of AT&T's woes can be detected, according to Burlingame, in the first deal completed by Armstrong, the merger with TCG in January 1999. TCG comprised a set of local channels to businesses and the concept was that it would become a platform for AT&T growth and greater direct access to business customers. The merger was intended to integrate "any distance" service to businesses in New York, Chicago, Houston, Boston, Milwaukee, and Fort Lauderdale. By reducing AT&T's dependence on the Bell companies for direct connections to businesses, the merger, AT&T said, would bring competition to the local services marketplace, giving customers "simplicity, convenience and choice—one-stop shopping for local and long-distance services."

The TCG merger was quickly followed by a mega-merger with TCI, another deal for which there was a sound stated strategy. "By weaving TCI's powerful, broadband cable network with AT&T's Worldwide Intelligent Network," AT&T announced, "the company plans to deliver integrated telephony, entertainment and high-speed Internet access services and a host of new communications capabilities to customers."

After the TCI deal was announced, AT&T's stock fell about 12 percent from the day before the announcement. AT&T next completed an acquisition of MediaOne, a Denver-based cable operator, in a cash and stock transaction valued at approximately $56 billion. The two cable acquisitions made AT&T the leading cable television operator in the nation. And Armstrong was certainly among the most acquisitive CEOs.

The Wrong Fit

Deals that seemed to make sense strategically produced results ranging from disappointing to disastrous. While many analysts have focused on the strategy and financial aspects of these deals, Burlingame emphasizes the cultural and execution elements.

Using the first merger with TCG as an example, Burlingame pinpoints where he believes the initial problem lay. On its face, the deal presented major hurdles in cultural terms. In a nutshell, AT&T was known as a buttoned-down, centralized, traditional large organization, and TCG was "very freewheeling." Being thrust into the AT&T culture frustrated TCG people, who "felt they got squeezed into AT&T," recalls Burlingame, "and some of them were given positions and responsibilities, others were not. Within a year and a half we had lost a significant amount of the human asset value of the acquisition. They had been a frisky little entrepreneurial outfit, very much accustomed to doing it their own way. They suddenly were folded into the big network organization of AT&T, and the whole life they had experienced in their past work environment changed. They didn't want to be a part of it. They ultimately found ways to demonstrate that there was constructive termination and so forth, and within a year and half, two years, they were out of there."

The basis of the troubles with the TCG acquisition—and later with TCI—says Burlingame, was that "very little accommodation was made for the success requirements to realize the dream of the acquisition. It was a deal and follow up was done purely on numbers, without understanding what was behind the numbers. There wasn't enough time, attention, or understanding of these deeper dimensions—culture. We didn't have an enlightened management that could understand that you had to do as much due diligence on the human systems and platforms required to make this thing work. They didn't realize this was as important as investigating the basic technology and the financial dimensions of the deal."

The end result was disappointment. Deals that should have worked, for which there were solid strategy-based objectives, failed because of the lack of integration of management teams. Leadership in the company, managing the acquisition, and overall communications began to break down because of a lack of clarity about who was responsible for what. This aspect was particularly apparent in the aftermath of the TCI deal.

The sad irony of the AT&T–TCI merger was that it held a great deal of promise from a business perspective, and managers further down in the organization were enthusiastic about the prospects. "Down in the organization they got it," recalls Burlingame. "They knew what had to be done; they were excited about it. The middle management and the front-line management people said, 'this could be great. And here's how we can work this thing out.' They wanted to make it work. But you had political forces in the upper levels and, of course, the repercussions trickle down three levels. Everyone else takes their cues from those at the top; it permeates the entire organization."

Subsequent deals were undertaken with a similar lack of accounting for prospective merging cultures and planning how to get the most out of each to achieve needed synergies. "It's not difficult to see the pattern here," says Burlingame: "totally underestimating the compatibility of the cultures and the capacity for people to team, to work together on problems. In addition, there was a complete lack of understanding of what core infrastructure, human and technical, is required to be in place to make things work."

The CEO's Perspective

The CEO's view is likely to be the most comprehensive, so it is bound to differ somewhat from anyone else's in management, even those who may be part of the top management team. Even prior to the extensive series of mergers he executed while CEO of AT&T, C. Michael Armstrong had acquired a great deal of experience in the realm of changing corporate culture; he was well aware of what a mammoth and time-consuming task it can be.

"Cultural change takes time," he observes, reflecting on his experience at Hughes and earlier at IBM. "I have never forgotten an experience that really drove this home to me when I was the director general of Europe, Africa, and the Soviet Union at IBM. I had taken on a project when the Iron Curtain was still strong, working to get IBM personal computers into the Moscow public school system. In the end, we were quite successful, and I had a wonderful luncheon, one-on-one, with then president of the Soviet Union, Mikhail Gorbachev. This was at a time when he was trying to define a new Soviet Union economically and all these economists from the U.S. were running over there each year helping him with his new five-year plan. During the course of our conversation, I said, 'Mr. President, how long do you think it will take before the people of the Soviet Union are producing a competitive economy?' I thought I was going to get a definition of his latest five-year plan, but he looked at me quite seriously and said, 'Mr. Armstrong, an honest answer is several generations.'"

The contrast from the five-year plan concept being invoked to transform a socialist-communistic economy to a market-based economy struck Armstrong. Gorbachev really understood the nature of cultural change. Although five years is the mere blink of an eye to some observers, Armstrong says, it may seem like forever to the analyst from the Street whose frame of reference is a mere ninety days.

Cultural change was a high priority when Armstrong led Hughes. "America had won the Cold War," he recalls, "and our aerospace defense business, where our market was the government, was probably cut in half." As a result, Hughes had to completely redefine itself, from a single-customer orientation—the U.S. government—to a competitive, commercial organization. "Here was this marvelous aerospace, defense, satellite, and technology company, probably the closest thing to a national laboratory that existed, and now it had to become a commercial enterprise serving, not a single customer, but thousands of business customers."

Change of this magnitude requires not only time, says Armstrong, but the right training, and a lot of it, including inventing and implementing the right metrics so people know whether they are succeeding by the new definitions of success in the new environment. There are a number of dimensions to cultural change—the arithmetic, the market logic, and the emotional—and all need to be addressed.

In the course of the Hughes transformation, Armstrong became acutely aware of cultural differences within the organization that would affect training and adaptation to the new environment. At that time, scientists, engineers, and technicians made up some 50,000 of the company's 80,000 employees. "We had an outstanding technical organization but finance was not in their blood, not in their vocabulary, so we invented a measurement called RONA (return on net assets) because it allowed us to capture both the balance sheet and the income statement. When we were about halfway through the training on this, I visited a laboratory outside of Washington and the director, a brilliant Indian scientist, greeted me and said, 'Mr. Armstrong, it is so nice to see you here but I do not see that Rona is with you and when I meet her I know I will be happy to see her as well.'"

Maintaining Cultural Independence

Training and integration proceeded at a different pace by unit, depending on individual subcultures, when the organization faced a vast culture shift. Armstrong recognized the importance of keeping particular operations separate from the rest of the organization to maximize their effectiveness. When he was at IBM, he says, the chairman had the wisdom and foresight to separate the company's effort in the personal computer business into a completely distinct organization—in its physical space, metrics, and compensation. Allowing it to create and maintain its own culture was critical to success and was driven by its own unique market. It was, in effect, a division of the mainframe business. "It was important that this new culture be compatible with the new market, the new product, the new services, the new software," he explains, "all of which were going to be different from the existing culture. So when I started the DIRECTV business at Hughes, I did not want it to be simply an outgrowth of the satellite business because what we were going to be in was the broadcast entertainment business. So I housed it in a separate building with a separate measurement system, a separate compensation system, and a separate management team so that it could grow its culture to adapt to the market rather than trying to adapt an existing culture to the market."

Recognizing the importance of allowing some cultural differences under the umbrella of the main organization was a key part of the initial integration strategy for mergers when Armstrong came to AT&T. "I never had tried to integrate TCI or MediaOne into AT&T," states Armstrong. "I made a very conscious decision not to because the business was different, the culture was different. The markets could be defined as common with AT&T because we both served consumers, but I never had them reporting to me and I did not have them reporting to the president who had the mainstream consumer network and business operations. Because we had to bring voice and data communications to the infrastructure, I did put several people into these operations from AT&T who knew a lot about how to do that but would also allow it to maintain a separate organization. I did not view the cable operations as belonging in what I would have defined as the AT&T/Bell culture.

"I wanted to make sure, as in the case with DIRECTV and with the personal computer, that the real integration would be to bring telephony to the infrastructure and then subsequently to bring on MediaOne so we had a critical mass. My whole strategy was to build a national broadband company and we got two-thirds of the way there when we had to restructure in order to finance the future. And so for those who might want to poke at me for not integrating TCI and MediaOne into AT&T, from the first day of the closing, it was never meant to be integrated. I'm a great believer, when it comes to culture, technology, and market, of leading from strength, and what the cable guys did well was far different from what the telephone company did well. In order to get telephony into that infrastructure, I did not want to have to put up with the cultural change."

Chapter 2 Planning Checklist

Assessing management teams in a merger situation is not an easy task, but the rigor and depth with which it is undertaken may well foretell the overall success of the match. Beyond the facts and figures that may indicate a good match, careful attention must be paid to corporate cultures and how they are likely to mesh. Otherwise the union is likely to come unglued at some point because of irreconcilable differences. Following are a few critical issues to maintain focus on:

1. **Set merger objectives early.** The objectives of the merger should be clear to management from the start. Plan to establish a list of specific objectives linked to a schedule early on as a way of measuring progress and critical junctures and determining whether the merger is remaining on course in terms of the original plan.
2. **Choose managers who are believers.** Managers must understand the reasons for the merger, as well as buy into the transaction and be prepared to evangelize on its behalf.

3. **Involve operational leadership.** Mergers are not just about strategy. They require the insight and executive capacity of operational leaders to make them work. Every merger plan should involve executives with operational experience in evaluating and carrying out a merger.

4. **Establish top management early.** A successful merger requires that senior leadership—including the CEO—be established early on in the process. It is much more difficult to bring the CEO and his or her team in later on and expect them to have the same passion, or understanding, for the deal as those who dreamed of it.

5. **Understand that corporate culture is key.** The CEO must understand the critical role of culture if the deal is to succeed. The message trickles down from the top, and if the CEO can't see beyond the numbers and implement programs and procedures to facilitate integration, it will never happen.

6. **Include human resources as part of the team.** Companies that understand the value and critical role of the senior human resources executive are likely to be more successful at merging cultures. There are many established best practices that can be implemented to help ensure successful integration, and the merger team should take advantage of them.

7. **Understand the CEO's motivation.** Some CEOs love to do deals and have less regard for the practical aspects of making sure they fulfill their promise. The board should provide a good check on the CEO and make sure the company is undertaking a merger for the right reasons and has the proper support to succeed.

8. **Value more than one culture.** Recognize when intraorganizational cultural differences are critical to the success of a strategy and may necessitate carving out cultural niches to separate parts of the organization from the whole.

□   □   □

When companies know where they stand on the human capital front, who possesses the right mix of skills going forward, they can begin to execute their human capital plan. It will be critical to spell out a clear vision of what the new organization will look and feel like, both at the 100,000-foot CEO level and for the troops on the ground. In the next chapter we will examine companies that have had success, as well as those that have not, in executing such a vision and the consequences that followed.

CHAPTER 3

Create a New Vision

■

Those who are directly involved in mergers often kick themselves afterward for not having seen what in retrospect seems
abundantly clear, particularly regarding day-to-day compatibility. But in the rush of excitement over a deal, it is often hard to
focus on anything beyond the business, the numbers, and
anticipated synergies.

John McCartney,
vice president of Datatec, Ltd.,
and president and COO of U.S. Robotics
when it was acquired by 3Com in 1997

Announced in January 2000—and approved by the FTC
in December of the same year and by the FCC a month
later—the AOL Time Warner deal had the distinction of
being the biggest merger in U.S. history. Just three years
later, the deal has been judged a disaster of mammoth pro-
portions. Virtually the entire top management team has
resigned; the company posted a nearly $100 billion loss in
2002; and it faces U.S. government investigations into its
business dealings as well as institutional shareholder lawsuits
alleging the company inflated its stock price by overstating
revenues.

Executed at the height of the Internet boom, the merger was
to be a perfect marriage of old and new economies. Long-
established Time Warner would provide content while relative

upstart, the technology-driven AOL, would provide the needed access and delivery to customers.

The merger certainly suffered from the worst timing imaginable, considering the bursting of the Internet bubble a mere three months after the announcement, which made the economics of the deal unsustainable. This fundamental problem led to a litany of other problems that began to sabotage the merger almost as soon as its planning got under way.

In addition to the insurmountable economic stumbling blocks there was a culture clash, which alone would have threatened the existence of the new entity. AOL's much younger, more arrogant management team, while technologically savvy, had relatively little tried and tested business experience. Time Warner's team, by contrast, was much older and far more traditional in its approach to running a business. As would become apparent later, it was almost impossible for one to coexist with the other.

The net result is that AOL Time Warner now serves as the poster child for how not to undertake a merger. The economics have proved disastrous, and the company did not move swiftly enough to resolve culture and management conflicts that have further exacerbated an already dire situation.

The major challenge when two companies come together, whether in a hostile takeover or a merger of equals, is not the issue of one culture overtaking another. The challenge is to construct a brand-new vision of a third, entirely separate company—the combined entity. What will the company look and feel like? What sort of organization and management team will it need to be successful? All questions, of course, lead back to the projected strategy going forward and all of the elements required to support it.

Bruce Ellig began at Pfizer in 1960 as a personnel generalist and retired at the end of 1996 as head of the company's human resources function reporting to the chairman and CEO. He knows a great deal about what it takes to build a successful corporate vision. For his last twelve years at Pfizer he ran the worldwide human resource functions for the company reporting to the chairman/CEO.

It is invariably a mistake, says Ellig, who is now a human resources consultant, to make a blind leap of faith, particularly with an acquisition. "Oh, they'll love working with us, we'll be supportive, and they'll be able to tie into our network. That all sounds well and good but many times, the individuals in question, say, 'the way I look at it, I've got several levels of organization above me that weren't there before and I don't find that very comforting.'"

If an acquisition or a merger proves to be the best route to follow (as opposed to an arrangement such as a joint venture, where two companies remain separate), there must be great care and thoughtful planning to ensure the merger lives up to its promise. In spite of the many cautionary tales and the wreckage from other mergers and acquisitions, says Ellig, "there are some CEOs mainly focused on building a much bigger organization and, in some cases, I think many of the key issues and key considerations don't even get addressed, much less thought through."

One of the most complex issues, he says, is corporate culture. "If you've got two organizations with different cultures, you've got a big problem. You have to ask the question, do you get any synergy from that type of situation? I don't think so. There are not many instances where organizations look at the culture issue early on. You have to identify what type of culture currently exists for this organization and what is going to remain. Unfortunately, very few organizations will pick the best of both and create a totally new one," an approach Ellig advocates.

"Corporate culture" is a catchall term that includes everything that makes a company unique. In addition to the mundane everyday realities of a corporation's workplace atmosphere—the rules governing dress, behavior, and communications that are internalized and may be little thought about—culture includes such fundamentals as:

- Decision making: Is it primarily centralized or decentralized?
- Metrics: How is performance, both company and individual, measured?
- Compensation: How are managers rewarded and what sorts of values are being reinforced?
- Technology: Is technology a tool or a central focus of the culture?
- Values: Is "how" results are achieved as important as "what" is achieved?
- Employees: Are they treated with dignity and respect?
- Focus: Is the company finance driven or marketing/sales driven? Is it driven by the top line or the bottom line?

With so many variables, a company's culture is unique and may differ radically from that of another organization in the same industry, making a merger of those two firms even trickier.

In the context of mergers, discussion of culture often revolves around the question of which will prevail. We believe this is the wrong focus; the emphasis should be more on creating a blueprint for the combined company and much less on the contest between corporate cultures. A delineation of the new company's strategy will help illuminate goals, objectives, and organizational personality as well as the kinds of managers who will be in harmony with the culture and will be a good fit in helping execute the strategy.

It is really not a question of interchanging or meshing cultures but rather of clearly defining what the new culture is. Leaders need to precisely define what the new operating environment, the new "corporate culture," will be: what is expected of people, how they are expected to behave, what the incentive compensation system will look like. Defining these variables accurately and crisply is key to having the right leadership team in place. And to a large degree, senior management will evolve based on a self-selecting process. Some people will be attracted to the culture and the vision that have been defined and others will not. The strategy comes first, then the vision that flows from it, then the operating environment, and then the managers and employees who will make it all work.

The Troubled Merger of 3Com and U.S. Robotics

Leadership is one of the most crucial elements in establishing a new vision of a combined company after a merger and in getting the company on solid footing, asserts John McCartney, currently vice chairman of Datatec, Ltd., a $2 billion networking products and service company headquartered in London. Prior to his current position, McCartney was president and COO of U.S. Robotics. After it merged with 3Com, he was president of the combined company's largest unit and cohead of 3Com's merger team.

His experience at 3Com taught McCartney a few things about what it takes to succeed in the corporate marriage game. One of the most important things, he says, is "extremely resourceful and creative leadership by the CEO of the combined organizations. My view is that if you are honest and upfront about what you want to achieve then it's the CEO's job to make sure those goals are attained. He has to be dynamic, and to some extent ruthless, about making sure that happens. You have to say, 'this is what the new organization is trying to achieve and this is how we are going to do it. And if you're not on board with that, you're gone, regardless of how terrific you may have been in one of the prior organizations.'" He emphasizes the urgency of establishing a working definition for success in the new organization.

Hailed in the business press as a blockbuster merger, what analysts called the biggest networking deal ever, the merged company, 3Com, was built on a strong strategic foundation. The merger was negotiated in the first several weeks of 1997 and consummated on June 12, 1997. In announcing the deal on February 27, 1997, the *San Francisco Business Times* proclaimed:

> In the largest merger deal ever announced in Silicon Valley, Santa Clara–based 3Com Corp. will pay $7.33 billion in stock to take control of U.S. Robotics, based in Skokie, Illinois. The proposed alliance combines 3Com's computer networking products with the high-speed modems made by U.S. Robotics. Together, the companies have 12,000 employees, $5 billion in revenue and could one day dominate sales of modems and other equipment used to connect people and businesses to the Internet.

But the merger has not lived up to expectations. At the time of the merger, the companies were comparable in size; 3Com was a little bit bigger, with $2.6 billion in revenue compared to U.S. Robotics' $2.2 billion, and a little more profitable, while U.S. Robotics was growing much faster. But the net result of the transaction has been a significant depreciation in shareholder value. Following the merger, 3Com significantly underperformed the technology market from the date of the transaction to the end of 2000.

Mergers, says McCartney, generally fall into one of three general categories. "One category is the merger of equals, where that really is the intention, but it rarely works out that way. The second category is when one side thinks that's the intention, and the other side doesn't at all. The third category is when neither side believes it's intended to be a merger of equals, but they both decide that should be the PR spin, either because it's the best way to convince Wall Street that the merger is a good idea or it's the best way to retain employees over the short run. In the 3Com–Robotics case, I think that both sides went into this feeling it would be a merger of equals and that we would be able to eliminate the relative weaknesses of both companies and create something much, much stronger than either could have alone."

According to McCartney, both companies were able to sort out very quickly some of the things that tend to be stumbling blocks as they put the deal together. In the course of about a week, before the deal was signed, major issues were resolved, including who the CEO would be, what the name of the company would be, where the headquarters would be, and who would run the major units. From an ownership standpoint, it was pretty close to a fifty-fifty deal. "Both sides had a pretty clear understanding of why we thought it was a good deal," says McCartney, "and I think that the top management team from Robotics was very business and financially oriented. And if a structure made sense in terms of what we thought the returns would be, we tended not to let ego get in the way of deciding to do it."

What began as a well-engineered, rational process went off course when the new company felt the impact of outside forces beyond its control. The deal began to founder for a number of reasons, not the least of which was that market conditions for the two businesses changed very dramatically immediately before and right after the deal was consummated. But while unfavorable market conditions made it tougher for the new company from the start, the biggest challenge, says McCartney, was the inescapable fact that the companies were very different culturally.

"I think it's very difficult to accurately assess those issues," says McCartney, "in a situation where the companies have not been romancing each other for a long time. It's actually not dissimilar to a job interview. You're meeting with a number of people, over a relatively short period of time, and you have to make an assessment of them, and, in this case, their organization. By the nature of these transactions you don't have the opportunity to delve deeply into the guts of the organization. An incredible amount of time gets spent on financial, and often structural, issues, but it's very difficult to get a sense of the culture and the personality of the company. So, you're basically making those decisions based on your assessment of the people you're working with in structuring the deal. And in some cases that doesn't accurately reflect what the rest of the organization is like. It's almost impossible to accurately gauge how individuals operate, how the companies operate, what the processes are, and how people have been trained, either formally or informally, to behave. You don't see that until you're in the trenches working and that doesn't come until long after the deal has been negotiated."

The cards are stacked against abandoning the deal after announcement and before close. So, adds McCartney, if you encounter challenges during that critical period, there is tremendous momentum to continue with the merger because the consequences of walking away for either party can have such severe financial repercussions. Consequently, there is a predisposition to push down potential problems and assume they will be resolvable.

Roadblocks to a Common Vision

A smart CEO in a merger will recognize the need to forge a new identity for the new company, and actively construct a new paradigm for success going forward. Messages from the top should leave little room for ambiguity or misinterpretation. Those who are not a comfortable fit with the new culture will either leave voluntarily or perhaps be laid off, enabling the new company to get off on solid footing.

"Overall you could calibrate the big differences culturally by describing 3Com as a very profit-oriented, tightly planned and controlled, engineering- and product-driven company with a strong disposition to avoid confrontation—very internally focused. And I would characterize Robotics as being very entrepreneurial to the extent of being freewheeling, extremely aggressive, customer-focused, relatively decentralized, and not only tolerant of confrontation but actually fomenting it. I can make that assessment in hindsight; I couldn't necessarily do that up front. If you really want to get down to it, you could contrast them as one being cerebral, and the other being street smart."

There was no systematic effort to define success in the new company in terms of the new strategy at the outset. As McCartney tells it, the lack of human capital assessment and lack of any real integration effort had disastrous effects. Within about a year from the start of the merger, virtually the entire Robotics top management team had left, and because of the way their compensation had been structured and related human-capital issues, mostly of their own volition.

"The senior management of Robotics," explains McCartney, "had substantial equity interest in the company, and we had followed a policy of being very generous with the equity in the recruiting and growth process. So, to a large extent, the senior executives at Robotics were already quite wealthy. And the transaction allowed Robotics executives to accelerate their options vesting (more on compensation issues in the following chapter). So if it wasn't fun, exciting, and challenging any more there was no reason or need for the Robotics executive management team to stay. And I think, independently, people one by one decided it wasn't really fun."

Some organizations are probably not destined to merge successfully, but others, with the proper assessment of human resources and the ability to assemble a team that matches the new strategy, can access those goals. Above all, doing the homework up front, before the deal closes, is critical to a desirable outcome.

McCartney firmly believes that if the right steps had been taken to identify and retain talent, the outcome of the 3Com–U.S. Robotics merger might have been much happier. As cohead of the 3Com merger team, he strongly advocated hiring an outside organization to assess various layers of management and provide counsel on benchmarking and whom to select for key roles. But others on the integration team disagreed, saying it would be threatening to managers.

Though U.S. Robotics and 3Com were certainly contrasting cultures and integrating them was a stiff challenge, we sensed a certain regret when we spoke with McCartney, a feeling that if more effort and care had been taken to surface potentially volatile issues early on and resolve them, the outcome of the merger might have been successful.

It is often hard to pin the blame for a failed merger on one variable alone; transaction and follow-through are complex, multilayered processes and outside forces may have a major impact. In the case of 3Com and U.S. Robotics, for example, by the end of 1997, the broader economic context was already taking its toll. "Tech News" on CNET.com described the company's woes this way:

> The newly merged company already had been facing problems stemming from financial tumult in Asian markets and the ongoing industry battle to agree upon a standard for 56-kbps modems. Now, a shareholder lawsuit taking issue with the company's temporary discontinuation of shipments is threatening to take even more oomph out of the revenue boost that USR's modem business was expected to give 3Com. The conspiring of events adds to the trouble 3Com has experienced as a result of decelerating growth in demand for networking products, which led to the company's decision to ratchet down shipments to the channel in an attempt to move to a more "just-in-time" shipment strategy.

The news story chronicled the slide of the company's stock. Given the shaky industry environment at the time, could the merger have succeeded in any case? It's impossible to say with any degree of certainty what might have happened, but it seems likely that it would have stood a far better chance of success had the human capital and cultural issues been approached more astutely and systematically.

Pfizer Warner-Lambert: A Fair Process in a Hostile Takeover

The 3Com–U.S. Robotics merger was a friendly marriage but failed to achieve its anticipated potential. Mergers under more difficult circumstances would seem to face an even tougher road. A hostile takeover can play out in a number of ways as far as the culture is concerned. Employees of the target company may feel angry and dispirited, leading to an exodus of the talent that presumably made the company and its products or services attractive in the first place. Conversely, leadership of the new enterprise can send a clear message to employees of both companies: Regardless of which side of the fence individuals are on, everyone will be given a fair shake in a systematic, impartial process geared to aligning talent and skills and not to political maneuverings.

Under somewhat difficult circumstances, Pfizer chose the high road when it took over Warner-Lambert. In the company's press release issued February 7, 2000 (the date the deal was signed), the headline read, "New Company to be Named Pfizer Inc., Will Integrate in a Spirit of Partnership and Mutual Respect."

According to Joseph G. Bonito, vice president and group leader of Worldwide Organizational Effectiveness & Consulting Services, the integration process was carefully planned and executed with detailed precision. It proceeded with remarkable alacrity from the February 7 deal signing until Warner-Lambert and Pfizer were officially operating as one company on June 19.

With more than a year's hindsight when we interviewed him, Bonito gives Pfizer pretty high marks for adhering to the principles intended to speed and smooth the transition to one company.

Bonito believes that the best ambassador for the new company was the Pfizer CEO Hank McKinnell. Contact with McKinnell, Bonito believes, increased everyone's comfort level with the merger. "When Warner-Lambert folks had the opportunity to meet with him, the reaction was,

'He's straight, he's honest, he says what's on his mind, he doesn't talk political doublespeak.' People would come out saying, 'I might not have liked what I heard, but he's straightforward.'"

Establishing the Right Structure

If the subject is performance-driven cultures, don't be surprised if the name Pfizer comes up. When McKinsey & Company worked with Pfizer, they referred to the company as the most "performance ethos" culture they had ever been exposed to. Pride in this competitive spirit runs deep at Pfizer.

The merger with Warner-Lambert was clearly intended to enhance performance rather than cut costs, the primary goal of many other mergers. "This was a top-line revenue-driven merger," says Bonito, "and I think that makes the difference in terms of the approach. This was not about cutting cost but about growing two very successful businesses. The tagline we adopted that puts the whole thing into the right context is 'the best get better.' Warner-Lambert and Pfizer were two of the fastest-growing pharmaceutical businesses in the last two or three years. And what we wanted to do was establish and execute an upside vision, which for us is about growth."

As part of its highly systematic approach, Pfizer distilled the essence of the integration down to a number of charts, which it used to disseminate the company's philosophy and goals. One of the charts, entitled "Seven Imperatives for Integration," illustrates the two companies linked together at the center with the caption "Successful Integration" surrounded by all the variables critical to this mission. Surrounding this core were the seven imperatives:

- Establish and execute against an upside vision
- Create the new pharmaceutical company/business
- Build enthusiasm among external stakeholders and in the market
- Identify and capture appropriate short-term synergies
- Build enthusiasm among Pfizer and Warner-Lambert employees
- Keep the current business running smoothly
- Consummate the deal

From beginning to end, the merger and integration of the two companies were planned down to the last detail. All issues critical to the merger were analyzed and a plan of action was developed with specific goals and targets to hit along the way. The superstructures and complementary substructures were also established within the organization to ensure accountability for each step of the merger and its attendant objectives. Little was left to chance.

At the top, an integration steering committee, comprising top executives from Pfizer and Warner-Lambert, was set up to oversee the merger. Then, within each major business unit—pharmaceutical, consumer, research and development, corporate—there was a series of design teams. An integration support team, comprising a group of executives the next level down from the top, which included Bonito, was jointly responsible for the real coordination work.

"Usually there is one integration manager; we had three," Bonito said. "Structurally we set up an integration coordination team and in each one of these areas we had about twenty-five to thirty integration teams, each led by the line leader, and then by the appointed integration coordinator. That coordinator was responsible for managing the integration process, ensuring that deadlines were met, ensuring that there was collaboration. For example, in the sales group, the sales integration coordinator, marketing integration coordinator, and the finance integration coordinator worked very closely because they are very interdependent. And then, corporatewide, we had a lot of other integration teams: human resources, communications, IT. So we had the top leadership team, the integration coordination team, and integration teams within individual groups and key functions."

This complex matrix that Pfizer set up to manage the integration of the two companies after the merger would pay dividends in terms of efficiency and productivity in the long run.

A Timeline and Deliverables

Once the management structure was in place to handle the integration, Pfizer next decided what tasks needed to be accomplished and what the timeframe was for each. The integration process was actually a series of complex steps, each a process in itself. The integration team set up a timeline called "Key Milestones." Each point on the timeline marked a significant juncture in the process representing that certain imperatives had been accomplished internally and could be announced to the public. Bonito described this as a cascading process, from the initial announcement of the merger on February 7, 2000, to the close on June 19 and the welcome meeting for the newly combined company the following day.

After the announcement of the merger, the first critical mark to hit on the timeline was less than three weeks later, issuing the "Guiding Principles" for integration that had been agreed on by the two companies, which included the following:

1. Lead the integration through Pfizer line management (functions and countries), coordinating decisions at all levels where necessary and leveraging a common approach and best practices.
2. Move quickly and predictably with intelligence, and mitigate risk.
3. Be transparent, objective, open-minded, and fact based.
4. Communicate decisions once they are made in a consistent, accurate, and rapid manner across the organization.
5. Base the integration on Pfizer's values with respect for Warner-Lambert: integrity, innovation, respect for people, customer focus, teamwork, leadership, performance, and community.

Integration proceeded apace, with new developments and announcements planned every few weeks. By March 15, the real heavy lifting commenced as the thirty-five integration teams began their work, and on April 18, the top leadership team of the combined company was announced. Following these initial developments, the two companies held their individual annual shareholder meetings, and the approval of the merger first by Pfizer's shareholders and then by Warner-Lambert's paved the way for the additional integration work that would make one company out of the two distinct entities.

After formal shareholder approval from both companies, leaders of the thirty-five integration teams began to take responsibility for merger integration. By April 27, the teams were charged with coming up with their deliverables, which fell into four main categories:

1. A description of all the tasks that would have to be accomplished on "day one" (the first day the two companies would formally operate as one company).

2. What the blueprint would be for the organizational structure going forward.
3. What the combined budget would look like.
4. Recommended best practices that would help achieve
   desired synergies within the new organization.

These deliverables would be presented to the board before
the formal close in June. Since the deal would close at the end
of the second quarter, Pfizer wanted to ensure that everything
was in place so it would also be able to close the books for the
quarter. In addition to the other pressures and deadlines to be
met in a merger, there was the additional wrinkle of demands
placed by the industry. "Since we are in the medical pharmaceutical business, you have to make sure that regulatory
requirements, including safety and adverse events, are properly documented. We are responsible for making sure these are
reported within twenty-four to forty-eight hours."

The challenges in this sort of a merger seem endless. Meeting the demands of the merger integration is one thing, but
there is also the need to carry on with the demands of business
as much as possible or the merger might succeed while the
business goes under. The needs of customers must be met and
there are the ongoing tasks of manufacturing, selling, and
shipping new products.

An evolving company in the throes of merger integration
needs to manage employees so that people understand whom
they report to as the company evolves. CEO McKinnell made
it clear that he did not want any "lost employees" as a result of
the merger. He wanted all employees to know what they were
responsible for and whom they reported to. To guard against
employees getting lost in the shuffle, he asked integration
managers to map every person in their business: who they
were, what they were responsible for, and whom they worked

with. He didn't want people showing up the first day after the merger not knowing what to do.

Cultural Roadblocks

Although both Warner-Lambert and Pfizer were highly successful, innovative companies, their distinct personalities presented particular challenges in merging them. Pfizer was mindful of these challenges and was particularly concerned about losing attractive Warner-Lambert talent. Warner-Lambert had adopted a poison pill provision some twenty years earlier. A number of preconditions, among them change of control, working for someone else, job change, and compensation change, could trigger a golden parachute for the top one hundred to two hundred executives. Moreover, even if they accepted the change, they had six months to change their minds. "People had a lot of money on the table," said Bonito.

To add to the difficulties, there was the issue of relocation. The new company would be headquartered in New York City. This was a radical shift for the Warner-Lambert team, which had been based in suburban New Jersey, and many were far from thrilled about it.

Bonito describes significant contrasts in culture between the two companies. Warner-Lambert had more of an open, communicative culture and was more paternalistic. The company was well known for its elaborate talent-planning process, including development of international executives. Because this was not billed as a merger of equals, there was no actual obligation to accommodate the Warner-Lambert employees. But Pfizer did not want to lose valuable talent and tried to make rational, sound business decisions about whom to keep in the new organization.

There were three big businesses that needed to be combined: the pharmaceutical business, the consumer business, and the research and development division. Depending on one's perspective, the transaction could look like a takeover or something more akin to a merger of equals.

"When you're talking about a multibusinesses company, it is not just an acquisition or a merger of equals; it has elements of both," said Bonito. "Pfizer had a very large pharma business and Warner-Lambert had a medium-size one, so we acquired them. In the case of the consumer business, it was just the opposite, and Warner-Lambert subsumed Pfizer. In the area of R&D it was kind of equal, and there it was more like a merger. So the top leadership in pharma is just about all Pfizer, top leadership in consumer is much more Warner-Lambert, and top leadership R&D is about sixty-forty. But when you're talking about a multibusinesses company, it is not just an acquisition or a merger of equals; it has elements of both."

Courting and Identifying Talent

As Bonito suggested when considering Pfizer's report card on the merger with Warner-Lambert, communication is key to success. Even in the case of a hostile takeover—maybe even especially in such a circumstance—communicating with employees and letting them know what to expect each step of the way may play a crucial role.

Marc Feigen is a partner at Katzenbach Partners, a consultancy that "helps enterprises achieve peak performance by offering distinctive capabilities that integrate strategic problem solving with insight into people and organizations." He says communicating is therapeutic and increases the comfort level of all involved. It is also an effective way of squelching rumors that can run rampant and breed on the high level of anxiety in the merger environment.

"My theory is that if you give people the opportunity to voice their concerns, you can then address them. What will the new culture be like? What will it take to succeed there? What are the chances of being fired? If the merger entails a move to a new location, there will be a lot of concerns related to that. People have to know that they will be heard and that there will be some sort of fair process in place to determine their fate."

Companies often worry about losing the managerial talent that can be the main attraction in a merger or acquisition. Having worked through these issues with client companies, Feigen offers advice that boils down to the following: Identify talent early, then make sure they are on board and understand and share in the new vision.

"The biggest lesson is to identify the people with the most knowledge, those you really need to retain for a successful merger as early on as possible. And they are not always the most visible people; you need to dig beneath the surface. They may be people down the line who are quiet in character, the ones people know are the go-to guys for resolving certain kinds of tough problems. It may be because they've been there a long time or they're just very smart," Feigen says.

"But the important thing to remember is that, to a senior executive who just bought the place, this person is invisible. They are going to know the people who wield the large bullhorns. But there will be lots of people who have talent, knowledge, and institutional memory who you're going to lose if there is a hemorrhage, an exodus of people. And that is why a thorough assessment of talent is so important. A good assessment will reveal that the people who make the most noise are not necessarily the greatest contributors. And when you identify those you really need to hold on to, you want to get a good retention package into their hands quickly."

Companies must be willing to court those they really want to keep and then bring them into the fold. People have to learn about the new opportunity ahead of them and become excited about it and those they will be working for.

Feigen points out that holding on to talent after a merger is an adverse selection process. "The most desirable people with the strongest résumés start marketing themselves first, and those are the people you want. Then you've got people down the line who may be high performers, but they're younger. They're saying, 'Oh my God, my mentor, my boss just left,' and they start looking. Not only do you lose the good leaders, but you also lower the morale of the up-and-comers if you aren't prepared to take quick action to stem possible losses. A knowledge economy where your people are truly your assets can implode very quickly."

The Acculturation Process

After a deal is done—whether an acquisition or a merger of equals—how can companies ensure that people, including new hires, have a clear idea of the new vision and are integrated into the new organization? Niko Canner, another partner at Katzenbach Partners, helps clients with "onboarding projects" designed to pull the workforce together after a merger by ensuring a shared vision and alignment of goals.

"We believe the critical part of the merger is this integration. There is always a large number of people who need to be aligned with the new vision and what precisely it means to their work. Often many people leave, and extensive hiring also necessitates heavy integration work," says Canner. Although the broad vision may be articulated by the CEO, what does it mean in day-to-day operational terms to those in, for example, marketing? The corporate vision is by definition broad enough to encompass many different departments and initiatives.

In the course of onboarding projects, Katzenbach Partners works closely with clients' human resources to help develop the general architecture to integrate new people. This integration phase includes:

- Initial communications before a person is brought into a specific group
- Giving people the new "vocabulary" (as opposed to specific job-related skills) they will need to succeed in the company
- Substantive orientation to help people develop the new abilities they will need to fulfill their new role
- Developing ongoing social supports (mentoring, peer clusters) people will need to integrate into the company culture

The goal is to help new or acquired people become embedded in a network of relationships so that they feel and perform as part of the fabric of the company and are aligned with the company's goals at the level at which they are operating. Building cross-functional groups helps strengthen communication and the warp and weft of the corporate fabric. Companies that have completed an acquisition and hope to keep incoming talent and new hires might benefit, says Canner, from having several meetings a year initially, across organizational boundaries, about concerns in the new company that people will need to think about.

Added support to the overall integration architecture will increase the odds of successful acculturation. Such support, according to Canner, includes designating an individual who is accountable for the success of each new person and providing information systems that help novices navigate the new company, such as an internal website, and organized orientation and welcome meetings.

The trick, says Canner, is applying the general integration architecture to different levels of the organization: "You have to build the process and customize it to functional or business groups. While an outside consultant can do much of the work, to be truly effective, you need the support of an internal function (human resources) that can reach out and cultivate the internal client relationships. The initiative on the part of human resources lends legitimacy to the exercise and ensures a custom fit."

Ideally the parts of the architecture needed to facilitate the integration will already be in place. Building on already existing supports and relationships—and perhaps reconfiguring them to fit a new purpose—is much more effective and efficient than building from scratch.

Integration and assimilation after a merger should not be viewed as a monolithic process. Tailored solutions vary from company to company as well as, particularly in larger organizations, from one business group to another. As the corporate vision and the definition of "success" are pushed down through the organization, it must be made clear to employees at every level what their goals are and how their day-to-day activities reinforce them.

"Because of the nature of what they do," says Canner, "some groups will just naturally be further ahead in this area." He gives the example of one client, a pharmaceutical company, in which the marketing function could more easily capture what they do in their particular area. The worldwide marketing head quickly articulated five basic principles, which helped mobilize marketing and enabled the group to communicate its goals to a variety of audiences. "Other functions are simply more diverse and the messages more diffuse," like the medical department in the same company, "so attaining this sort of focus is more of a challenge."

Chapter 3 Planning Checklist

Forming and disseminating a new corporate vision that is distinct from that of either of the two companies that are coming together in a merger or after an acquisition is a critical first step in creating a cohesive and ultimately successful new entity. The message must first come from the top and be broadcast throughout the company and to the outside world, explaining what the new company intends to be and to stand for.

The following checklist of items should help effectively communicate the new company's vision:

1. **Articulate a vision from the top.** The CEO must articulate a vision of what the mission and values of the new company will represent to employees and customers.
2. **Spread the word fast.** Rapidly communicating the new vision throughout the merging companies can alleviate anxiety and stem the loss of valuable talent. Employees must understand what the change will mean to their individual jobs.
3. **Identify critical managers.** Find the talent critical to retain if the merger is to succeed.
4. **Court employees.** Especially in knowledge-based industries, losing talented employees is the same as losing business assets. Court them as ardently as you court customers.

5. **Create integration teams.** A network of integration teams starting at the top of the organization and spreading throughout the company's various functions, equipped with timelines and specific goals, can help accomplish a smoother integration of the merging companies.
6. **Communicate, communicate, communicate.** Even when the news is not good, employees will appreciate knowing the score and being able to plan their own lives.
7. **Minimize cultural friction.** Establish an "onboarding" plan for those who will stay and those who will be added to the company to ease the transition.

□   □   □

Once a vision has been articulated, the company can more clearly identify the management team and other employees who will best fit into the new scheme and will be able to forge ahead to achieve the business goals set out in the vision. Recognizing the keepers—those critical to success going forward—is critical, as is determining how to hold on to them during a period of flux. We provide some guidance in the next chapter.

CHAPTER 4

Retain and Motivate Key Players

∎

The less-effective organizations in mergers don't pay enough attention to the human resource; they just focus on numbers. They don't realize that in order to execute any strategy, in order to win in any marketplace, you have to have the people who can go to the Superbowl.

Robert J. Stucker, president and senior partner,
Vedder, Price, Kaufman & Kammholz

There are a number of distinct and complex challenges associated with mergers and acquisitions, some of which we have already examined, including taking stock of human capital and deciding on the leadership and the overall vision and specific strategy of the new enterprise. One of the most difficult challenges is holding on to talent during the limbo period: the time between the announcement of a merger and the date when the two companies operate as one. This can be a protracted period, particularly in a regulated industry, and smart companies will do everything in their power to lock in valuable talent and ward off competitors and recruiters who can lure talent away during this vulnerable time. Managers may see the chance to move from an unsettled environment to a stable one as very appealing.

What can companies do to protect themselves, both internally and externally, when a primary consideration is stemming the loss of human talent? First, find out how competitive your compensation system is. Employees who feel underpaid or undervalued will be the first to walk out the door. At no time is it more important than now to make sure you are completely up to date on the latest compensation and benefits developments.

Companies that have been diligent about doing their homework will be in far better shape as the merger progresses and they need to have the new company's team in place. That means having sought expert advice on a couple of fronts: (1) in ferreting out executives who will be key members of this new team and (2) in having the most effective compensation and benefits packages in place to ensure that these executives will be there to help launch the new company.

High Anxiety

The limbo period when the company is going through change, whether it's integrating another entity or a full-scale transformation, is a time of high anxiety for all involved. Even executives who are assured of landing on their feet are likely to be uneasy. Operating executives may watch as plans they may have been working on for years are put on hold, perhaps permanently, and skepticism about how this new combination will work out may be rampant. It may be easier for executives on the ground to spot serious potential trouble spots than for two CEOs who are mapping out top-level strategy at 100,000 feet.

For those planning the actual transition, there is a different sort of stress associated with deciding the fate of others in the company. When someone who has been a great, loyal warrior for years is ushered to the door, everyone, including those who had to terminate him or her, feels the impact.

But this is not the time, no matter how tempting it may be,

to make decisions based on emotion or personal relationships. Companies that resolve to work within a logical decision-making framework will emerge much stronger. The ultimate result will be more palatable for all involved, even for those who may not be selected for precisely the position they wanted. People who perceive the rules and the process as fair are much more inclined to accept the outcome, even if it is not all they had hoped it would be. Companies can lower the risk of alienating those who remain by making sure that severance packages for departing collegues are fair.

Eye on the Vision

Although companies must keep track of strategic, cultural, financial, and often regulatory issues during a merger, the key focus from start to finish must be on the vision for the new company, and how everything else fits into it. If top decision makers on the integration team can maintain a steady focus on the strategy for the combined company, an evaluation of the people needed to execute the strategy and operate the company from day to day will naturally follow.

An atmosphere of confusion and insecurity inevitably sets in among all employees immediately following the announcement of the merger as people become anxious about if and where they will fit into the new scheme. The CEOs of the two companies must be prepared to sketch at least a broad outline of what the new company will look like, the purpose and the values it will represent, and what the employees' mission will be.

In planning a merger, those at the top sometimes focus so intently on repercussions affecting the value of the company and the reaction of Wall Street that they forget about one of the most important constituencies: the employees of both companies. By selling the vision of the new company and engaging managers, encouraging them to stay put at least for the time being, the integration team can buy time to have the luxury of making decisions about who will stay and who will go. This will be a critically important and time-consuming task as the new company strives, with as much accuracy as possible, to select a management team with skills that match the needs of the new company.

In buying time, especially with those managers the new company would likely want to keep, communications tools can be just as important and effective as financial tools. Any information that can be conveyed to key managers about their roles and responsibilities in the new entity that helps ground them and gives them a greater feeling of security will be essential. Retaining talent is more of an issue today than ever before.

The often-repeated McKinsey-coined phrase, the "war for talent," isn't just a buzz phrase; it is a reality. Our day-to-day experience with client companies, combined with a steady stream of data, indicates that leaders are in short supply. Companies that lose a significant percentage of their leadership, whether through negligence or inability to properly communicate and nurture relationships, may find it impossible to recover. As we have said throughout this book, the success of a merger—any merger—rests on the skills of the management team that will execute the strategy. The loss of management assets can have a disastrous effect on the merger's prospects.

The Merger's Raison d'Etre

During a merger, companies that lose a significant percentage of their leadership, whether through negligence or inability to properly communicate and nurture relationships, will be starting with a huge deficit.

Properly categorizing the business case for a merger helps determine who stays and who goes, and helps define what incentives will be needed. Roger Brossy, founder and principal of compensation firm Semler Brossy Consulting Group, says that generally the raison d'être for the deal can be put into one of three buckets:

1. **Economy of scale**, which entails broadening geographic scope, may be the objective, when companies merge or acquire one another to complement each other's reach in new and key markets. Part of the goal will be to shrink the infrastructure dramatically and reduce redundancies.
2. **Leveraging a core business** may entail redefining the overall business and strategy. An airline, for example, may decide to leverage its capabilities to move into car rental companies and hotels, buying into businesses that are either further ahead or further back in the supply chain.
3. **Transferring skills or technology** is the main point in mergers where companies acquire or merge with companies to advance their product line to be on the cutting edge of developments in technology.

Once it is clear what the business case is, says Brossy, the retention objectives should be much more clear. Viewed through the lens of the business case and the overarching rationale for the merger, the human capital imperatives should become apparent and give companies a picture of who they will need to hold on to, what financial incentives will be appropriate, and who will be less critical going forward.

To aid clients in developing a retention strategy and the tactics to support it, all of which will be consistent with the merger's business goals, Brossy uses the following framework and asks a series of critical questions:

- Clarify retention objectives:
  How does the retention effort support the merger's business case?
  Retention for how long?
  Retention for what? To stay? To perform?

- Identify key employees:
  Where do we focus our retention efforts?

- Establish timeframe:
  What are the critical events?

- Install retention vehicles:
  Do we first address the fundamental pay system?
  What about add-on vehicles (cash, equity, phantom equity)?

- Monitor and adapt:
  Are retention plans achieving intended goals?
  If not, what can we change?
  Are goals realistic?

All roads lead to the strategy, the business case. Evaluating the importance of individuals in the organization will first be determined by how critical their functions will be going forward and then by an individual evaluation of those in high-priority areas. While those in top leadership positions (the CEO and the senior executive team and business unit heads) are perhaps the most visible, there are other equally critical positions in a merger, particularly in knowledge- or product-intensive industries. Without the key players in these functions, whether focused on product development and innovation, customers and markets, or capital markets, the merger will not approach expectations.

To keep an eye on the ball, and avoid developing an insular perspective, Brossy says it is important to continue to listen to the market and to remember what merger goals, and thus retention goals, are.

"The merged company is presumably worth more than two stand-alone companies. Why?" asks Brossy. "The acquisition premium theoretically puts a dollar amount on the unrealized value, and it's important to be mindful of how that value will be unlocked. If that value is based on cost savings, it will be critical to reduce expenses; if it's based on growth opportunities, the company needs to be increasing revenues; if it rests on investment opportunities, the goal will be to find alternatives to internal capital investment."

Once the rationale for a merger is clearly understood, the partners will want to "create a common blueprint for the new entity, the merged company," says Lance Berger, head of Lance A. Berger & Associates, Ltd., which serves a wide range of clients in the areas of change management, human resources, and compensation." If it is an acquisition, you will still be revising the blueprint and getting people to share in a common vision. The blueprint is a set of assumptions that link the mission, vision, strategies, goals, culture—the sum and total of the company—into one place. And a critical aspect of that coordination is making sure that the strategy, the operations, the culture, and the reward systems of the organization are aligned."

Identifying the Keepers

Job one after a merger has been decided on—even before it has been publicly announced—is to establish a comprehensive, consolidated human capital plan that is congruent with the mission of the new company, the overall vision and strategy, marketing and financial goals, and culture. These elements are all cut from the same cloth and must not only be consistent but also help reinforce one another. Within a human capital plan, the very distinct and precise messages a company sends through its compensation proclaim what the company values: entrepreneurs or bureaucrats; long-timers or up-and-comers; all-business or family orientation. A compensation system that is well thought out and thorough will accurately reflect a company's culture.

The first step in implementing a plan for the new company is to carefully assess the talent on board; who goes and who stays; the value to the company of those who stay and where they will be positioned; and where bench strength must be fortified. A human resources expert can then help design a system that carefully reinforces just what the company would like to accomplish.

"The organization must determine who the high-potential employees are, who the high performers are, the people they can't lose who are in the critical positions," explains Berger. "That becomes one of the key elements of the input into the reward system, which is basically a way to place selective premiums through the compensation system. Once you have decided on what your human resources or human capital plan is, the compensation plan will help you retain those who are important to keep, including those who may be blocked in positions and need to move out."

A talent assessment will help identify the gems in the company—hidden or otherwise—as well as those who are less important to future success and those who will be redundant under the new regime or may even prove a barrier to success.

It is important to get an objective market value of the worth of each person the company wishes to keep. In order to do this it is critical to gain a perspective from outside the company. "We need to determine the individual's market value, what competitive levels the company chooses to compete at in that pay market, and what should be the mix of compensation, that is, base salary, annual incentives, long-term incentives, stock options, grants, and so on," explains Berger. "Once we know that, then we begin the process of selectively putting people on pay programs based on their performance, and their potential in the organization." With a clear idea of each individual's competitive level in the overall pay market and ongoing importance for retention, it should then be relatively straightforward to modify various elements of an appropriate pay package.

Of course, it's not all about compensation. Ensuring that those who will be valuable to the organization, those who are currently high performers—and those with high potential—stay on entails more than guaranteeing them an appropriate level of salary and benefits. Equally important is continuing to communicate their place in the new company and painting a picture for them of what their future will look like.

It is not enough to identify the real talent; a company must work closely with them to court and keep them. The success of the new enterprise depends on it. People who once saw a path to the top of the corporation, for example, may now see that path blocked by another executive performing the same function. Duplication is inevitable in a merger, and allowing a confusing or ambiguous situation to continue is a mistake that many companies make. It is an error that may have serious consequences. The longer it is allowed to continue the greater the anxiety within the ranks and the greater the likelihood of mass defections, leaving huge holes to be filled in the organization.

Those with the most in-demand skills and experience, the ones companies would most like to hold on to, will be the first to land on their feet somewhere else. The very reasons these executives are attractive to one company are the same reasons a competitor will be all too happy to snap them up. And competitors and recruiters are just waiting in the wings to snare them.

Creating Appropriate Incentives

Designing appropriate incentives to retain key executive talent is driven by the business strategy going forward, and packages that are offered may vary greatly depending on where that person is located in the organization, the relative importance of that unit, and the relative importance of holding on to that individual compared with his or her peers.

All retention decisions and tools should emanate from basic business decisions and motives, says Brossy. Assessing an individual's value in the total scheme of the merger and beyond is critical, and a number of important questions must be answered to provide the required information for these assessments.

"Think about segmenting management populations the way you might think about segmenting customers," says Brossy. "For example, you may very clearly want to retain the line personnel, and you might want to keep the executives in Asia and Europe, but perhaps those in the U.S. are redundant. You may want the infrastructure or the staff jobs: IT, accounting, finance, HR. Then you must try to identify the way the process is going to work: What are the critical events? Is it going to be hostile, and if so what's the likely time frame? What are the various stages of the deal from announcement to closing? Once all that has been determined, as much as possible, you put in the retention vehicles to support the plan."

Even before a merger may be contemplated, most large companies have severance plans with "change of control provisions." Typically, the top five named officers, those who appear on the proxy, are viewed as valuable company assets and are provided a significant package to ensure that, regardless of what happens, these folks will be well taken care of. If one of these individuals is terminated as a result of a downsizing from a merger, this normally triggers the change of control provision and the executive is compensated according to his or her severance package.

As we have noted, it is always those who are the most valuable to the company going forward who will be the first to leave as well as to secure another position. It is therefore imperative to have a plan in place to retain them, at least until the new company gets over the hump.

An executive who stays on after the merger for a year or a year and a half may leave the company voluntarily and collect his or her severance package. Most change of control provisions state that the executive must stay for a stipulated period of time to be eligible for the severance package.

Compensation specialists who advise clients on these transactions help identify the players—the brains behind the product or research. In knowledge-intensive industries, such as pharmaceuticals or software, this is critical. And if a company that is being acquired has a legacy technology system (one that will be in use after the acquisition is completed), planning had better include retaining the executives who have the know-how and experience to run and maintain it.

Be sure incentives include both the monetary and the non-monetary variety. The financial incentives may be fairly straightforward, though they will vary somewhat depending on an individual's value to the company. But it is also important to communicate individually and directly with each of these key human resources to ascertain how they view their future. How do they see their career and what do they hope to accomplish? If the goal is to keep these executives in place, they must understand their importance and feel assured that their desires are being heard, understood, and integrated into the future of the new company.

Not by Compensation Alone

Compensation experts we consulted all emphasized that much of what motivates people to remain with a company during the disruptive period following a merger has little to do with compensation. Roger Brossy cites studies of groups of executives. When asked to rank a dozen issues related to considering an outside job offer, pay ranked below the top ten considerations. Many other issues factored more importantly into the decision, including the quality of one's boss, job security, financial stability of the company, challenging assignments, and decision-making responsibility and authority.

Executives who will be important to accomplishing the merger and helping achieve the new vision must be cultivated and rewarded, like any important resource. There are financial, psychological, and social components to the gestalt that makes up the "total rewards strategy," as Brossy puts it. The constellation of variables that revolves around this strategy includes direct and indirect financial rewards, such as salary, incentive compensation, and ownership, as well as benefits and perks. But today many executives care equally, if not more, about career and quality of life issues, including those that may have an impact on their families.

Of particular significance during a merger are affiliations; people's attitudes about where they will be working, how they fit into the new scheme, and whom they will be working with become critical issues. People become emotionally tied to a company, a brand, and what it represents to them, and they have to have faith that the company that will be superceding it will also fulfill those emotional and psychological requirements. People want to feel pride in their association with a company, and this psychological payoff can be as significant as the financial payoff. The company that employs them is, in many ways, a reflection of them and their values. If the corporate and individual consciences are out of synch, there will be a problem in keeping capable managers and keeping them motivated to want to do the best for the company.

An Expensive Proposition

Since implementing sophisticated retention vehicles can be a financial drain on a company, such tools must be used judiciously and usually are limited to the most critically important senior executives, on whom the success or failure of the enterprise going forward may indeed rest. Below the most senior level, where redundancy may be a greater problem and skills may be less specialized and in demand, retention plans are usually replaced by severance packages, which are more straightforward and far less costly to the company.

"Golden parachutes" were first deployed during a high-volume period for mergers in the 1970s. The underlying philosophy was that key executives, if assured a soft landing regardless of what ultimately happened with the company, would focus on what was good for the company rather than saving their own skin.

Retention agreements have grown increasingly sophisticated and can be prohibitively expensive, including not only payouts that amount to multiples of an individual's salary but also extensions of health benefits, including postretirement, vesting of stock options, and financial counseling.

These agreements have grown more complicated because of the desire to hold on to talent. Simple agreements include one trigger, typically "change in control" ownership transfer that allows executives to take the money and run. In these cases companies may find that managerial talent required to make the merger succeed has marched out the door.

Compensation specialists help clients construct retention agreements that are appropriate to the specific individual, how much he or she is valued in the organization, and to the specific goal—to retain the individual for the long or short term or merely to ensure that the intelligence he or she leaves with is not used for the benefit of competitors.

After the strategy is illuminated, the options are a veritable Chinese menu, the primary variables being the executive's worth to the organization and how much the company is willing to spend as a result. How much does the company want to retain a particular individual and for how long? Perhaps whether someone stays is of less importance than the fact that he or she may have trade secrets that the company does not want to get into someone else's hands. In this case a noncompete provision may be in order. If integration is the goal, the company will need six months to a year to get through shuttering plans that will not be moving forward, identifying redundancies, and transferring customers. Stabilization, on the other hand, requires a more flexible and open-ended time frame, likely at least a year. According to this scenario, the goal is to ensure that people don't retire on the job or go into limbo because of anxiety over the change instead of focusing on performing their jobs well.

"Formal employment agreements tend to be limited to senior executives and might include such provisions as a two-year noncompete in exchange for stock options, guaranteed salary, and possibly a nonsolicitation provision," says Brossy. Stay bonuses are also common and may consist of a cash payment or a stock award. Employment agreements may include any or all of these elements; the more elements, the more potentially expensive a proposition to the employer. After Aetna merged with U.S. Healthcare, for example, the seven "critical executives" were awarded five-year contracts and guaranteed salary and target bonuses, restricted stock, and sign-on cash awards at the time of the merger.

Deferred cash accounts, says Brossy, are another retention vehicle. Companies may deposit cash in accounts and establish a vesting schedule that allows them to retain key executives and retention targets for a period of years.

There are a number of stock-related techniques companies can call into service, each with its own advantages and disadvantages. Unvested stock options may be a dicey issue in the entire menu of retention vehicles, but there are several formulas compensation experts can employ that work to preserve the equity represented in these options, essentially ensuring that the option holder remains whole and that the option term is preserved. Restricted stock is yet another option and, though it must be used more selectively than stock options, advantages include immediate and understandable value, high perception value (if stock is strong), and the fact that fewer shares are required to transfer value. "To compensate for vesting restrictions," says Brossy, "as a sweetener, companies can pay tax liability upon vesting." There is also the possibility of a phantom long-term incentive plan, which he says may be the best way to preserve the entrepreneurial spirit of the acquired company while encouraging retention.

Retention Vehicles: Pros and Cons

VEHICLE	ADVANTAGES	DISADVANTAGES
Deferred compensation accounts	• Can be performance based • Tangible account balance • Preferable tax treatment to participants	• No tax/accounting advantages • Administration
Restricted stock	• Immediate, tangible value	• Less shareholder friendly • Taxable event at vesting
Phantom LTI plan	• Linkage to value creation at business unit level	• Complexity

Source: Semler Brossy Consulting Group

A Strategic, Tailored Approach

It would be difficult to overemphasize the importance of maintaining focus on the vision of the new company going forward and those who will be essential to the success of that enterprise as well as on what the company will be willing to do to hold onto these critical executives.

"The successful mergers will do more analysis at the front end as to who they want and who they do not want, and will determine, even with those they want to retain, is it realistic to expect them to stay on?" says Robert J. Stucker, president and senior partner with the Chicago-based law firm Vedder, Price, Kaufman & Kammholz, which advises corporations and individuals on a broad variety of corporate and commercial matters. The firm has a national reputation as the premier firm for executive compensation and employment matters.

The best outcomes of mergers, claims Stucker, result from the right legwork, approached as methodically as possible going in, and individually tailored plans apply to staff and operating executives alike. "Interview them, talk to them, qualify them, find out about what their thinking will be post merger. What will their commitment be to their career and what will be the timing and the design consistent with that? Post closing, make sure they are integrated. Check back with them and see if are they doing well. Integration and melding, developing a one-team approach, does not happen automatically. It has to be worked and managed just like other aspects of an organization."

Like the other experts we have interviewed during our research, Stucker laments the fact that too little time and effort is often expended on getting the human element, the new company's engine, right in a merger. "I think smart CEOs of big surviving companies understand and are sensitive to the human resource element. In addition to the time they spend negotiating the purchase price and operational aspects, they know they have to invest equally in exciting and motivating the team that is going to come on board. People need to know that they are going to be a vital part of the team and be treated accordingly. If you are treating them like some territory that has just been conquered, you are doing yourself a disservice, because every day that group can find a way to be dysfunctional in terms of merger integration," warns Stucker.

Regarding incentives and compensation to retain key players, says Stucker, the actual elements may be less important than what is perceived as consistent and fair by the employees. And the critical question is, of course, will the plan help achieve the desired results? "All of the elements—whether we're talking about stock options or restricted stock, the supplemental pension program, or treatment as a retiree eligible under various benefit programs—need to be looked at and designed on a basis that is consistent with the surviving company and how they normally do things. Also, will they motivate the kind of performance and the kind of deliverables that you want to get from that group, individually and collectively? So if there are certain types of costs that need to be taken out, or certain kinds of integration, set those as the drivers and make rewards contingent upon that because you usually get what you reward and recognize."

Integrating two vastly different corporate cultures, perhaps one entrepreneurial with a compensation system to match, and the other quite the opposite, can create intense challenges related to compensation and incentives. We asked Stucker, "How do you reconcile a situation like that?"

A big part of the solution in such a case, observes Stucker, is not trying to force-fit organizations and cultures with compensation systems. "I think the way you reconcile it," he says, "is not through compensation but through recognition of the differences and trying to perceive what the attitude is. You have a group that is going to be coming in, and there will always be resisters that do not want to get with the new program, do not want to drive for the common good. With that kind of individual it is always 'us' versus 'them.' Unfortunately in most mergers you have that kind of difficulty. So, you need to identify those who will not carp about their newfound friends as some kind of Martians from outer space, but are willing to work together. And you need to separate from the fold those who just cannot get on board. I think that it is easier said than done, like a lot of aspects of human resource management. The execution is very difficult because you are dealing with human beings and they are very complex. It can be a big mistake to assume just because we set up the proper pay programs that people become team oriented and support the new enterprise." To the extent that the acquiring company has pay practices and employment practices that are a lot sterner or stiffer than the company people are coming from, the acquirer should carefully examine these and determine if they are going to be out of synch and troublesome.

For example, he says, suppose you come out of an organization that has annual stock options that vest over three years, and the surviving entity is going to five-year cliff vesting (i.e., the entire stock option is subject to forfeiture until the fifth anniversary). "That is going to stick in the craw of a lot of executives who are bound to say, 'this is really Mickey Mouse, they can fire you in four years and eleven months and you will not get any of your equity awards.'" Perhaps more importantly, this will indicate to employees that the new company is not enlightened or user-friendly in its pay practices. Before you know it, Stucker adds, this difference in pay approach will be a daily topic of conversation among disgruntled executives who will become convinced that they are being treated unfairly.

"To the extent you do have those different types of pay practices, you need to understand that it's going to be like sand in the gears, and if there is any substantial difference, the acquiring company should see whether or not they can make adjustments to eliminate that source of discontent. Or if they are going to insist on doing it their way, figure out who is going to be able to embrace the new way of doing things, and who is just going to be a festering sore and never really come together with the group."

Compensation practices reflect a company's general culture, and determining the right practices and the right mix are critical to getting the merger off to a solid start as a cohesive team. "There will always be outliers," says Stucker, "the we-them people, and to the extent basic things like compensation are different you increase the percentage of outliers. Especially in an area that is more personal to them, they feel they are getting gypped in terms of how the system operates and how it is structured, creating a negative attitude about the company and their future there."

If drastic changes in compensation are to be implemented, the enterprise should not only explain the analysis but also sell its reasons for why it needs to work that way. In a competitive and normal company, says Stucker, you can explain things like this to people; you can point out to them how perhaps their prior world order was just out of synch with reality. "This is what the rest of the world does," he suggest. "Just look at these six companies; they are wired just like this too and you know, like it or not, we are in a competitive environment." People will understand, Stucker says, but reiterates the fact that whatever the compensation, world-class companies will lock in "A" players with super compensation.

Chapter 4 Planning Checklist

Retaining and motivating talent are significant challenges as companies emerge from a merger or acquisition, and the toll the entire process can take on employees at all levels should not be underestimated. Following are some steps companies can take to hold on to critical talent.

1. **Manage anxiety.** Recognize that the period of limbo between merger announcement and closure is a period of high anxiety for all employees, those who will stay as well as those who will leave.
2. **Clarify the vision thing.** Knowing what the "business case" is for the merger is crucial to making appropriate retention and compensation decisions.
3. **Align human capital and strategy.** Decisions about whom to retain and whom to terminate should be based on what skills will be required to make the merger work and attain the new vision.
4. **Tailor incentives.** Implement appropriate incentives tailored to whom should be retained and for how long (short term, medium term, long term).
5. **Create a culture statement.** Compensation and severance packages speak volumes about a company's culture. Make sure you are you sending the right message.
6. **Follow the golden rule.** If you expect people to operate as part of a team, treat them as human beings, not acquired territory.
7. **Aid understanding.** If drastic changes must be made in compensation practices, clearly communicate the rationale to employees so they will understand.
8. **Emphasize what goes around.** Create a rational system for

retention, termination, and compensation and make every effort to treat people fairly.

9. **Realize that people make it happen.** Remember, retaining and motivating the right people will help ensure the success of the merger.

□   □   □

Once employees critical to achieving the goals of the merger have been identified and an appropriate plan put in place to retain them, the real work begins. In the next chapter, we explore the myriad elements of integration, not merely of compensation packages but also of communications, systems, and procedures—all of the cultural elements that make each company unique.

CHAPTER 5

Integrate Deliberately and Swiftly

■

Do you want to know what's going on at a company? Talk to the people doing the work: They know. Talk to them yourself at breakfast or lunch or dinner or at the bar across the street. They know what we're doing right and what we're doing wrong. They know who is doing good work, who is a good manager, and who cares about the company. They also know those who play politics and look out only for themselves. Listen to them and learn.

Jamie Dimon, CEO, Bank One Corporation

In September 2001, Hewlett-Packard announced its intention to acquire Compaq Computer for $25 billion, the largest deal in tech history. In announcing the merger, Hewlett-Packard CEO Carly Fiorina and Compaq CEO Michael Capellas stressed the combined companies' ability to deliver managed solutions to large customers around the world, with a focus on storage, software, and services. Combining the two computer giants would create a company second only to IBM in size and global scale.

After a tough eight-month battle that included a proxy fight and a very public battle with company founders still on Hewlett-Packard's board, the Hewlett-Packard-Compaq merger finally got the go ahead in May 2002.

Though the new company had taken a big and difficult step forward, it was only the first of many required to create a successfully merged entity. The tough task ahead was anticipated by Fiorina when she said publicly, shortly after the announcement, "It all looks great on paper, but none of it will matter if we don't integrate successfully."

Indeed, the first year was devoted to a carefully planned and executed integration of people, teams, and businesses. There have been complex issues common to merging any two previously unique and independent cultures as well as issues related to a significant shift in the business model. Previously known chiefly for its products, HP is in the process of making a fundamental change to a service-centric worldwide powerhouse. While the company pursues other markets—including consumer, printing, servers, and mini-computers—its service and support to major clients will largely determine the ultimate success of the business.

Following a carefully designed blueprint for integration upfront should pay off as the company now stands poised to execute its new growth strategy.

Fight Ambiguity

Creating this sort of blueprint, then integrating the leadership team and functional heads is one of the most critical early tasks in a merger. Until the organization can rally around one leader and his or her team and internalize a clear message about what is expected, where things are headed, and what individuals' roles will be going forward, a company may remain in an indefinite state of limbo. Depending on how long this state lasts, consequences can range from mild to severe: from lack of clarity about mission and strategic goals to total confusion and alienation. This lack of focus may mean goals dreamed of in the merger's courtship stage may take longer to attain or may remain out of reach. Or the organization may founder completely, employees may become totally dispirited and disenchanted, and talent may bolt en masse for more seemingly stable opportunities.

"There are several elements that need to be put into place immediately upon announcement of a merger," says Ed Horowitz, former executive vice president for advanced development at Citigroup and founder of Citigroup's E-Citi unit. Horowitz is quite familiar with postmerger integration challenges from the inside.

"First, you need to take the most senior management of the company and provide them with a safety blanket that allows them to keep working and keep their minds open," says Horowitz. "For instance, if you had an organization of 10,000 that was created by a merger of two companies of equal size, you might take the top three hundred. That would represent the top leadership of the company that's responsible for driving the numbers because they run the businesses. You would want to put them under contract, probably for two to three years to give them a security blanket that sends the message, 'no matter what happens economically you're going to be treated with respect.'"

When people are not reassured about their future in the new organization, the results can be disastrous, derailing even a merger with the brightest prospects from a strategic point of view. If communications with key talent are less than optimal and executives are left in a state of uncertainty, they are particularly vulnerable to overtures about other opportunities. Even the most loyal and dedicated executives worry about their own future when that of the company is up in the air.

"Headhunters understand this period of transition, which is from a steady state to one of uncertainty, and it's the time they pursue your best people," says Horowitz. Having been through large mergers, he speaks from experience. "Those key executives are saying, 'I'm recognized as the best here and I've worked hard to get where I am. Now with this merger I don't know who's going to win. And the decision maker who wins may not know me and I may have to prove myself all over again. If I do have to prove myself all over again, I'd rather do it where I don't have to deal with all the turmoil that surrounds a merger."

Pfizer and Warner-Lambert: A Simple, Consistent Message

An important part of keeping employees on board during and after a merger and weaving people into the new organization is to communicate the purpose of the merger, what it represents, what the new army is going to accomplish. The message has to be simple—the merger boiled down to its essence—and repeated over and over in a variety of forums until everyone understands and internalizes it. It should become a rallying cry.

"Everyone tells you that communication is so important and boy is it," says Rob Norton, senior vice president of Pfizer's corporate human resources and head of human resources for Pfizer's worldwide pharmaceutical business during the 2000 merger with Warner-Lambert. "One of the things that we learned was that people are smarter than you give them credit for; they have to understand the rationale for the deal. Why are you doing this, why are you subjecting us to this trauma?"

This understanding, on a practical level, of the critical importance of ongoing communications during and after the merger led to a key element in Pfizer's integration strategy.

"From the beginning, we made a real effort to communicate goals and progress to employees," says Norton. "We stumbled at first; we had two different companies and two different philosophies on how to communicate. Eventually we moved to a third model where we had basically three or four consistent themes that we would hammer away at. And we would weave these themes into our communications on a fairly consistent basis. That helped a lot. Then we followed it up with an awful a lot of meetings with our leaders in front of crowds within the company. Sometimes, frankly, the crowds weren't all that friendly. People were anxious; they had lots of questions. So there was a great deal of exposure, allowing people to let loose at you, letting them ask leaders all the hard questions."

In Pfizer's case, this approach—central to getting people to buy into the merger—was made easier by CEO Hank McKinnell's firm belief in the value of the town meeting style of communicating.

"He's comfortable with it," says Norton, "and so you take the lead from that and if the boss can do it, everyone else can do it." In the end, people didn't always get the answers they wanted and not everyone was satisfied, but they did get answers to important questions and could assess where they stood. And that seems to have made all the difference.

In rallying the troops of the new organization, it certainly doesn't hurt to have a charismatic leader, but it is equally important to have a vision and goals that are understood and supported by all. According to Norton, those in the middle of the transition of the new Pfizer organization were pretty well tuned in to the message. The company did a lot of communications, he says, throughout the organization, and people took their cues rather quickly. Considering what was at stake for these individuals, they desperately wanted to know what the deal was and seemed to soak up the information, which was presented in a way that everyone would understand, although everyone may not have been happy about it.

Reflecting on his own experience in some exceedingly complex mergers and the issue of organization, Ed Horowitz believes "you have to be pretty straightforward, very consistent about what the mission is. You should be able to fit it on the back of a business card: three to five things you're trying to accomplish with the merger that are clearly understood and people can stick with. People don't assimilate the message unless they've heard it six times and so you've got to keep it going." In addition to clarity of message, says Horowitz, it is also essential to provide frequent updates—progress, where the organization stands in relation to the stated mission—and to celebrate this progress, as well as to admit failures, and move on.

Integrating Business by Business

One of Pfizer's mantras was "best people, best practice," a kind of jingle that was repeated constantly in communications during the course of the transition. This slogan is, of course, somewhat subjective, with the final determination of who was best suited for what role being made by the top decision makers.

"It became pretty clear that we were not going to meet everybody's standards in terms of who were the best people and what was best practice," says Norton, "and it came back to haunt us a little bit. But that's the way it works. The idea was that we picked the very best person we could for every job. We realized we were going to have to be more pragmatic about the transition, and so we gradually shifted the slogan to 'small into large, simple into complex.' That became something people could understand."

This approach helped Pfizer determine how to organize its

major businesses. Between Warner-Lambert and Pfizer, for example, Pfizer's pharmaceutical business dominated, so Warner-Lambert's was folded into that. In the case of the consumer health business, it was just the opposite, so Pfizer's business was folded into Warner-Lambert's. This approach made sense from a business continuity and risk point of view as well as from the perspective of employees, who perceived it as logical and fair.

People tend to think about merging monolithic structures, but it is important to note that companies, particularly large companies, are complex structures. And the complexities are magnified when you are talking about companies composed of distinct businesses, each with its own distinct culture. That is why the integration model developed by Pfizer—and accepted by its employees—that was ultimately so successful differed from business to business.

"Outsiders said, 'oh one big pharmaceutical company acquiring another one that's almost as big,'" says Norton. "But that didn't capture the nuances of the task. There was a consumer health care business, there was a confectionary business, there were very elaborate worldwide manufacturing infrastructures that had to be put together." In addition, there was a large number of corporate staff, some of whom had to be taken out.

As each of these separate integrations proceeded, there was a discrete model for that particular business or staff function. This discrete approach was also critical in communications, which were designed with the language of the individual's area in mind. Where one business could be folded into another, as previously described with the "small into large" or "simple into complex" philosophy, that was accomplished. In the case of combining R&D, however, Pfizer decided to totally redesign and reengineer something brand-new, the only example of that particular approach in the integration process.

In all, four to five separate and distinct models were used in the integration process, likely a key reason for the success of the merger. The process was perceived as a rational one driven by business objectives that were communicated to people throughout the organization in language they could understand—language that was not abstract but directly linked to what individuals were trying to accomplish on a daily basis. Lofty merger visions and goals are appropriately conveyed by the CEO. But when top human resources professionals are engaged in the challenging business of integration these abstract goals must be translated into operational objectives that are understood and appreciated by all employees, whether or not they remain with the surviving company long term.

Bank One: When the CEO Takes an Active Role

Jamie Dimon, who became chairman and CEO of Bank One Corporation in March 2000, knows a thing or two about merging companies. Perhaps most importantly, he knows two things about people involved in mergers: Most employees want to do the right thing and they desperately want to be proud of where they work.

For the past decade and a half, Dimon has been closely involved in some of the highest-profile mergers in financial services, including Smith Barney, Primerica, Shearson, Travelers, Salomon Brothers, Citicorp, and now Bank One and First Chicago NBD. Melding companies into a new culture requires discipline, hard work, decisiveness, and hands-on involvement from the CEO, sending a crucial message to the entire company. Ultimately the CEO must decide who stays and who goes, and what culture will emerge.

Dimon joined the executive suite in 1986 when Control Data Corporation spun off Commercial Credit Company, a struggling consumer lending business. As CFO and later president, Dimon helped define Commercial Credit's strategy and completely restructure the company. Numerous acquisitions and divestitures substantially improved the company's profitability, paving the way for the purchase of Primerica Corporation in 1987 and Travelers Corporation in 1993. Dimon served as president and COO of each company, and he took on the additional role of COO and later chairman and CEO of the Smith Barney subsidiary. In late 1997, he became co-chairman and co-CEO of the newly merged Salomon Smith Barney. A year later, Travelers bought Citicorp, and Dimon became the president of the new Citigroup.

In early 2000, Bank One's board was looking for an experienced—and hands-on—executive to succeed acting CEO Verne G. Istock, who had replaced longtime CEO John B. McCoy. The third generation of his family to serve as the company's CEO, McCoy had abruptly retired right before Christmas 1999. Seventeen months earlier, Bank One had paid $19 billion for First Chicago NBD, creating the nation's fifth-largest bank.

At 4:15 P.M. Chicago time on March 27, Bank One announced Dimon would run a company that had merged only on paper. Less than sixteen hours later, Dimon was at his desk on the ninth floor of Bank One's world headquarters in Chicago. Later that day, he met with all senior vice presidents in the company auditorium with telephone connections from around the world. On Thursday and Friday of that week, Dimon visited Columbus, Ohio—the company's former headquarters city—and met with executives, board members, civic leaders, and thousands of employees.

"Cultural issues are at the very heart of a successful merger," Dimon says. "We dealt with a lot of these challenges at Travelers and at Citi. There's a difference depending on the kind of transaction. Sometimes you don't have overlap that forces you to lay off people; then, the challenge is forming teams with your people. But it's all about good business logic.

"We did some big deals," he says. "Primerica, for example, was really buying seven companies all at once, and, of course, Travelers Insurance was a whole independent company. Perhaps the toughest ones of all were the boldest ones, where you had massive people, systems, markets, product, and customer issues, as we did with Shearson and then Salomon Brothers."

By the end of his first month at Bank One, Dimon had spoken with large meetings of employees in Bank One's major employment centers in Detroit, Chicago, Wilmington, Indianapolis, and Dallas. In Phoenix, he stood on the top of the dugout at Bank One Ballpark and told thousands of employees that he saw talent that could restore the luster to Bank One's terrific franchises—franchises that were threatened by pathetic customer service, hamstrung by multiple computer systems that didn't talk to each other, and weighed down by bloated costs.

Dimon likens merger integration to executing army campaigns. In fact, companies that execute mergers best literally have an army of practiced and professional staff that can spring into action on command. During mergers at Commercial Credit, Primerica, and Travelers, the army was primed, he says.

"They all would say the same thing to me, 'What time do you want me in tomorrow morning?'" Dimon recalls. "That group would include those who run marketing and sales, systems, operations, HR, treasury. Everyone would know exactly what to do because the army was really well trained. We all knew the drill because we had been there before."

"Once the routine started, there would be virtually daily meetings on a wide range of things, system conversions and all the people-related issues. All the system and people decisions would be made quickly," Dimon explains.

In his first year at Bank One, Dimon strengthened the management team by promoting talented managers and recruiting experienced managers. He fortified the corporation's balance sheet and saved Bank One more than $1 billion through waste-reduction efforts. He brought together all the company's technology executives, listened, and then dictated what computer system would serve as the core deposit system, to be called Bank One's Best, or B1B. Soon after, a schedule was created to integrate the five other systems into B1B.

The integration process was extremely demanding for Dimon personally because he sees no substitute for the CEO's involvement in critical initial decisions. At Primerica and Travelers, Dimon says, he was out every morning and every night getting into what he calls the "belly of the beast." "I insisted on taking people out for breakfast and dinner. At times, people on my side made me feel like a traitor, like I was going over to the other side, but I knew it was crucial to making things work."

Dimon used the same approach at Bank One, talking to employees at breakfast, lunch, or dinner. And he was no stranger to the bar at Nick's Fishmarket, the restaurant thirty feet from Bank One's front door. Every time Dimon visited a market outside Chicago, he made sure he had time for an employee meeting. In the summer of 2001, he began holding breakfasts once a month in Bank One's auditorium. He spoke for ten or fifteen minutes, then took questions for more than an hour. Employees never hesitated to tell him what was on their minds.

In a pressured postmerger environment, it is difficult to be viewed as fair. In one particularly heated exchange just before the merger of Shearson and Smith Barney closed, Dimon pulled what he calls a "Solomon." His Smith Barney people resented all the time Dimon was spending with Shearson's traders and senior people as he attempted to get to know their organization.

"They were saying, 'What the hell is this guy doing?'" Dimon remembers. "In this meeting, I finally said to the Smith Barney people, 'I'm tired of the stuff about Shearson. I want to get it behind me and so I've decided I want every single one of you to fire any three Shearson people you want and you can never complain again.' Suddenly the room got very quiet. One or two people started to clap; half the people took me seriously and the other half thought I was insane, but it seemed to help turn the tide from infighting to getting on to the more serious issues related to integration."

With all of the sophisticated evaluation processes and review procedures people normally associate with merger integration, the part that people forget about, according to Dimon, is the more qualitative element—what he refers to as the "breakfast, lunch, and dinner part." In the final analysis, however, this CEO believes that the cultural differences between merging organizations are sometimes exaggerated.

"Sure, there are vast differences between organizations," he says. "God, think of the difference in cultures between Travelers Group and Citi; those would be hard enough. But how about when you compare Travelers Group and UBS? Even so, these cultural differences can be blown out of proportion because you can find this sort of friction within the same group.

"Even if you have two identical genetic tribes get together, there's going to be a lot of fighting. Who's the alpha male? And that's how I think of it with organizations. Within the same group, there's a lot of jockeying for position. You deal with some of the most difficult human issues during a merger—being laid off or changing your boss—and the whole process can be so emotionally wrenching."

A Consultant's View

Merger integration from the perspective of a seasoned consultant who has observed and advised on many deals differs from the perspective of a CEO who has been knee-deep in a few. Jon R. Katzenbach, founding and senior partner with Katzenbach Partners, led the worldwide organizational performance and change practice of McKinsey & Co., for three decades. He brings valuable views and experience to the issue of merger integration. The author of several books related to his professional work, including the acclaimed *The Wisdom of Teams*, his particular focus is helping clients find the most effective approaches to leadership, team, and workforce performance, and to managing change in large enterprises.

According to Katzenbach, if two distinct organizations are to be successfully integrated, the actions and decisions of the people in those organizations must be in alignment. Alignment can be strengthened in four major areas: the structure, process, networks, and flexible units in the organization. Many companies work toward achieving alignment through the formal elements of structure and process but ignore the informal elements of networks and flexible units. Others, especially companies emerging from a venture culture, focus too much on the informal elements while ignoring the need for a more formal structure and set of processes.

In order to achieve alignment during a merger, the appropriate types of performance units must be in place. A performance unit is more than simply a group, he explains. It is a highly disciplined entity created especially to tackle a particular performance issue. A performance unit can be a single-leader unit or a real team.

Finally, it is up to the leadership group within the two organizations to enable the performance units and create alignment. The leadership group must include the right people who follow an approach that works for both organizations.

Formal and Informal Elements

The challenge of merging organizations is often approached by looking at the formal structure: who reports to whom, who is responsible to whom, and what the various boxes on the organization chart represent. Because structure is so familiar, definable, and concrete, it is the element that is most heavily relied on in almost any organizational design effort. "Certainly in merging companies, we worry about how to align those boxes and who is going to fill them," Katzenbach explains. Despite some recent writings about hierarchy and formal structure being a thing of the past, Katzenbach insists that it is foolish to ignore the value of formal structures and processes. "Once an enterprise reaches a certain critical mass and you are no longer able to rely strictly on personal interaction, you need to have a more formal construct in place to help make the system work."

If structure is the first of these devices, the second obvious grouping is formal processes or workflows that cut across the structure, for example, the planning process and the capital allocation process. Such processes are actually alignment mechanisms as well. They can help align behaviors in an organization by channeling information and workflows across the structure. Obviously, every company has both a structure and a set of formal processes.

"There are informal ways to strengthen alignment as well," Katzenbach explains. "This informal construct consists of all kinds of people networks and interactions. It also comprises organizational elements that I call the 'flexible units'—small groups, forums, task forces, teams, and other collections of productive people that are more flexible than formal structures or processes. These units are more easily assembled, focused, and disassembled to fit changing organizational needs. Because these units can be quickly directed toward a specific goal," he adds, "you don't have to go through the frustrations and potential disruptions of changing the formal structures or processes."

Formal + Informal Structure = Full Integration

Katzenbach believes that no formal structure works well without informal networks. "When you are bringing two institutions together," Katzenbach explains, "you are integrating two or more different cultures. Those cultures will have different sets of informal networks, some of which are more important to integrating and operating the combined entity than others. While it is impossible to map all of an organization's networks, it is worthwhile paying attention to the few that are going to be required for effective communication, work, and information flows. To some degree, these critical informal networks are totally independent of what you do with the formal processes."

Too often, however, companies focus entirely on the formal elements of merger integration, which leads to an overly simplistic and one-dimensional plan. A common trap in merger integration is thinking that organization is only about a formal structure and its processes; we shouldn't be lulled into thinking that this exercise captures all the important elements in aligning the decisions and behaviors across merging companies. "Structure," Katzenbach explains, "is only one of four major ways to strengthen alignment. While formal structure and process are certainly useful alignment devices, they are only one-half of the equation."

It is important to remember, however, that companies can "rely too much on the informal construct." According to Katzenbach, "this happens most often in companies that are emerging and are rapidly growing. Typically, they have come out of a venture culture where everything was informal, and everyone worked as an unstructured gang." After a growth spurt they may realize that this informal construct is not enough anymore; the organization needs a more formal structure to keep things running smoothly.

In sum, Katzenbach says, "when you merge two or more institutions to form a new organization, you should be addressing structure, process, networks, and flexible units in a balanced way. Otherwise, many of the critical elements of alignment will be neglected."

In the Interim: Different Teams for Different Tasks

Whenever you restructure an organization, the new structure typically works less well, at least in the beginning. In time, the new structure may be superior to the old, but initially it lacks the integrating benefit of a set of informal networks that were operating in the old structure. A restructuring invariably breaks those networks, and it takes time for them to be replaced by new ones. Unfortunately, informal networks can be very idiosyncratic within organizations. While you can try to accelerate the process and design portions of informal networks, you could never anticipate and design a total informal construct. "Business schools and organization experts can show us how to design a decentralized structure or a matrix structure," says Katzenbach. "But the informal networks that make the formal structure work just have to plant and take root themselves. That takes time."

During the interim, it is crucial to create a number of performance units to guide the merging activity, and to assign the proper performance units to the proper tasks. While various working groups are often created during integration, they may have unclear goals and lack structure. "A lot of the merging activity takes place under the guise of teams. The philosophy is to put teams together from both sides, to work on different aspects of integration," Katzenbach begins. "The problem is that multiple team performance demands a more rigorous approach than most merging efforts apply. The common assumption is that if you put groups together by drawing members from each side of the enterprise, they will learn to work together while accomplishing the merger task. Unfortunately, that completely misses the power of a performance unit.

"Ninety percent of what the world views as team effectiveness is nothing more than group effectiveness," he explains. "An effective group is not the same thing as a true performance unit; it is a group that simply communicates effectively and gets along.

"If you want or need a performance unit, you have to apply a very explicit discipline about the goals, the leadership role, and the accountability. Disciplined performance units are a hell of a lot better than effective groups, but they are not always necessary. They are really going to help you when you get the right one against the right task."

Single-leader Group or Team?

Katzenbach believes strongly that a successful merger can only be achieved by establishing the right kind of performance unit to accomplish the right integration-related task. The single-leader group and the team are two different types of performance units needed for the different tasks that must be accomplished. Both of those small groups are extremely valuable performance units in a merger, he says, but each serves a very different purpose.

A single-leader unit can be faster and more efficient, whereas a real team can be more versatile and offer greater leadership capacity. "The team discipline is different from the discipline that works best under a strong single leader," Katzenbach explains. "One is not better than the other; they are simply suited for different purposes. And if you don't get the right one in the right place, you will not optimize the effectiveness of the group and you will confuse those involved."

In order to understand when to use a team versus a single-leader unit during a merger, it is important to understand their strengths and weaknesses. A single-leader unit is a very efficient unit, and it's the right choice when time is of the essence and you have an experienced leader who "knows best" how to get the job done. Team building and team discipline take time, so if you don't need a team for a particular task and the time frame is tight, a single-leader unit, where one person is in charge (as opposed to a number of collaborators), is likely the right choice. When speed is essential, which is often true in getting off on the right foot at the start of a merger, the job calls for someone who has been around that track before and knows how to do it. That points to a single-leader unit. Furthermore, this is the unit we are most comfortable and familiar with in hierarchical organizations. While we may call them teams, says Katzenbach, they are really not.

On the other hand, you may have a group of people, all of whom have leadership capabilities that are relevant to the task they are assigned to. You may want more than one of them to be able to lead that unit if required. Relying on a single leader won't accomplish that objective. If you are facing complex problems and issues, and no single person knows the answer, then you want people who bring different capabilities and perspectives to the table because that's the only way you are going to get the optimum solution. In this case, a team may be the most useful type of group. "Both teams and single-leader units can function as powerful performance units when they apply the appropriate discipline to the right performance challenge," according to Katzenbach.

Leadership System: Starting Fresh

Having the right formal structure and informal networks in place is critical to meshing the two merged entities into one. These elements require the creation of performance units that can be tailored to their performance challenge. And the creation of performance units requires the right leadership team with the right approach to enable them.

"A senior leadership group doesn't work entirely through

its formal reporting lines and responsibilities," Katzenbach explains. "It has counsels, it has forums, it has different ways that executives come together, make decisions, and allocate resources. So one of the first things they have to figure out is how are we going to have two different cultures come together."

One of the first tasks of those charged with integrating during and after a merger is to make sure the right people are in the right jobs and to make sure the right sorts of teams are in place. "One part of the job is just making sure we have only one chief financial officer and we have only one chief technical officer, so what are we going to do with the others?" Katzenbach says. "A lot of time is spent deciding who is the right person for the right job and how do we put these various pieces in place."

Another equally critical element is determining what kind of leadership system and approach the new organization will need. Is it going to use the planning process of Company A or the committee structure of Company B? Or is it going to integrate the two approaches? To increase the odds of a successful integration, Katzenbach says, "when you are bringing two different institutions together, and two very different cultures and mind-sets, you really should take a clean sheet of paper approach."

The "clean sheet of paper approach" has clear advantages. You are not blinded by the biases of either organization; the assumption is that each has its pluses and minuses and that the strengths of one can complement and enhance the strengths of the other. Assuming that one structure is best often means losing what is good about the other structure. Yet those strengths are part of what contributed to its attractiveness as a merger partner in the first place. In addition, there will be a steep learning curve for one organization's executives to get over as they learn to function in a completely new structure. If there are compelling reasons for selecting one structure over another, these trade-offs make sense; if not, it is better to seek to integrate the best of both into a new structure. Otherwise, you can easily alienate people and undermine a successful integration. This is a particular danger in a hostile takeover. "Of all the things you don't want to lose these days, talent is the most precious. And that's the risk that hostile takeovers run," says Katzenbach.

Two important examples here are the GE-Honeywell near-merger and the Dunlap debacle at Sunbeam. "What would GE have done if they had merged with Honeywell?" Katzenbach asks. "They would probably have left Honeywell's structure in place, as long as they could see it operating separately. But once they found major areas where integration instead of simply independent effort was required, they would probably have absorbed Honeywell into GE's strong system. That may not have been the best way to do it. Perhaps they would have been better advised to form a new set of counsels and forums to take full advantage of complementary strengths of both companies."

Katzenbach recalls the heavily publicized story of Al Dunlap, Sunbeam's former CEO, as an example of how not to do things in this sort of situation. "The guy was incredibly open about what he was trying to do, but the approach was very disruptive. In the short term, was his approach a good way to straighten out a poorly performing business? Sure, because if you take out costs and you take out assets, you force simplistic priorities and guess what? It looks better. But you lose talent in the process, and you fail to build a winning company on the basis of systems and assets. If your behavior forces talent out, the consequences are not in anybody's long-term interests."

The right leadership group following the right processes is critical for a successful merger. During the crucial period of time when informal elements of the new organization are still being formed, an effective leadership group will be able to ascertain whether a team or a single-leader unit is better suited for a particular performance challenge. Meeting these performance challenges will enable two companies to align their structures, processes, networks, and flexible units in order to establish themselves as one integrated, successful organization.

Chapter 5 Planning Checklist

Among the essential ingredients of effective integration following a merger is a carefully planned, well-thought-out process, implemented and executed as quickly as possible. Here are some of the objectives companies should keep in mind, best practices that are recommended by those who have been around the merger track a few times:

1. **Create a leader with a message.** Without a vision, employees languish. A strong leader articulating a clear message is essential if the troops are to go forward with purpose and vigor.
2. **Fight ambiguity.** Leaders at every level of the organization should be determined as quickly as possible; power sharing in any unit for any length of time leads to confusion and works against achieving the best results going forward.
3. **Lock in key people.** Identify and lock in key people and provide them with a security blanket if the merger doesn't work out as planned.
4. **Have a rallying cry.** Communicate the vision down through

the organization until the message of the merger becomes a mantra.

5. **Customize the model.** Especially where distinct businesses exist in a merger, don't assume that the same model and message will work for each. Assume you'll have to tailor both.

6. **Put the CEO front and center.** There is no substitute for the direct involvement and judgment of the CEO in making and communicating critical organizational decisions.

7. **Realize it's all about alignment.** Integrating two companies is all about aligning missions, goals, strategies, and resources, and informal networks that support the formal structure are key to organizational success.

□   □   □

If the new company is to get off to a running start, the integration process must begin well before the new entity gets the green light to operate as one company. Assuming everything falls into place, that may not be enough. After all, the federal regulatory process can stall finalization of the merger or even bring it to an abrupt halt. This can create serious ramifications for companies that may have proceeded far down the one-company route with a competitor. More on this and other issues related to the regulatory process in the following chapter.

CHAPTER 6

Survive the Regulatory Process

■

It is something that will mystify me for the rest of my life.
David Fuente, former CEO, Office Depot
(on the failure of the proposed merger
with Staples to win FTC approval)

Ask anyone who has been through a merger—the CEOs at the top or employees at all levels who are expected to carry on with their duties—and you will learn that the most trying period is the limbo period after the merger is announced but before the two companies officially operate under one banner. So much to do but such an insecure time.

In addition to running their current company—guiding management to implement current strategy, manufacture products, serve customers, and perform myriad other responsibilities—CEOs need to plan the structure, operations, and management of the new, combined organization. Employees too must execute their responsibilities, often in an atmosphere of uncertainty and anxiety, unsure how (or even if) they will fit into the new order being planned.

How exactly do CEOs achieve the proper balance for planning, which is essential if the new company is to get a running start, but dicey, since there is always a chance that the merger will not proceed? Most of those we interviewed stated unequivocally that beginning to integrate as soon as the merger is announced is critical to the future success of the combined company. This leap of faith is worth taking, they contend, because lost time in integrating cannot be made up, and with so much to do before official "opening day," speed is essential. This optimistic and practical view must be weighed against the specter of the deal not going through at all. Even though companies receive signals throughout the regulatory process about how their deal is progressing, surprises can sometimes occur. And if the deal is scratched, companies may live to regret having gone too far with the integration process and having shared too much confidential information with a company that is no longer a potential partner, but rather an ongoing competitor.

Staples and Office Depot: Down the Garden Path

As we have briefly suggested in earlier chapters, the scrapped merger of Office Depot and Staples is a curious and cautionary tale about the risks of proceeding too quickly with premerger integration. Although it is difficult to determine precisely what should be deduced from this example—it may be more the exception than the rule—it is an important example of the possible negative repercussions of integrating too early.

After six years, Office Depot's former CEO David Fuente remains confused about what happened and why. "Early in 1996, Office Depot was working very hard to try and acquire Staples, and at that time we had a higher price to earnings ratio and Staples's was a little lower. We were able to put a transaction together that we were just never able to consummate. We had something of a setback financially and Staples had a particularly good quarter and our P/E ratios reversed and they offered to do the deal in reverse. In other words, have Staples acquire Office Depot. Basically, it was a transaction that I thought made a tremendous amount of sense. Our board agreed and they approved it, so we proceeded into the regulatory process."

Office Depot was no stranger to the regulatory process and its intricacies, having done at least ten previous mergers without the slightest regulatory issue. Everything had been approved in less than thirty days, and the CEOs had no reason to believe that the Staples–Office Depot deal would be any different. "In this particular case, we went through the same process. We were assigned to the Federal Trade Commission and went through the filing process. On day 30, we got a notice that the FTC decided to ask for a second review. But this was in no way alarming and the process still seemed pretty much a normal one. The FTC acted within their thirty days and they had certain deadlines after we filed our second and third requests for papers. Those were things that all seemed to proceed smoothly."

But the process began to get bogged down around the issue of market definition. While the FTC defined the market as "office supply superstores," which meant an extremely high market share, the two companies had defined the relevant market as "office supplies," which was a far lower market share and consequently much less of a problem. The issue of market definition continued to be a problem, expanding to include the efficiencies in the deal and the savings that would accrue in running one company instead of two.

The CEOs finally got the message, says Fuente, that the deal would be approved only if Staples sold off a grouping of their stores, and the only potential buyer was OfficeMax. This put a great deal of pressure on Staples to identify a package of stores that would satisfy the FTC and negotiate a deal with Office-Max before the FTC voted on the merger. "We were not able to make that deal and they voted for a staff recommendation against the merger and the commissioners voted to support their staff," says Fuente.

But the roller-coaster ride didn't end there. "We subsequently went back to OfficeMax, which was somewhat distressed that they did not get the deal done and missed a really excellent opportunity to enhance or change," Fuente elaborates. "We were able, again, with the assistance of the FTC's staff, to assemble a package that would please everyone. From our point of view, we had satisfied the staff, and satisfied OfficeMax, and made quite a sacrifice in the bargain."

The final blow, according to Fuente, after all the time and effort expended, was that "much to our surprise, the commissioners voted against the deal that their staff had negotiated and recommended. And off we went to court."

The precedent-setting effects of the final outcome are also disturbing to Fuente, who believes that the decision gives the FTC much broader latitude and greater judgment in market-definition issues in future cases. All in all, he says, not a very favorable outcome for business in general. All the more disturbing to Fuente is the fact that there were no warning signs along the way. The process and requirements seemed reasonable, though in retrospect, of course, a lot of time was wasted on a deal that did not go through, which negatively affected the operations of both companies.

Why did events unfold in such a bizarre and unanticipated fashion? Fuente is still clueless. "I cannot even begin to tell you why," he says. "It is just one of those things that happens, and I think that it was really a bad-faith exercise on the part of the Federal Trade Commission. It certainly was a real negative on the operations of our company and on the operations of Staples as well.

"And, I guess when all is said and done, I do not have the

slightest idea why those commissioners did not support their staff. There is no doubt that they were being guided by their commissioners in crafting this deal. I do not know whether the commissioners got mad at somebody in the deal, if they hated our attorneys—that would be easy to understand! Essentially, they turned down the deal that they had crafted for us."

What is particularly ironic, Fuente says, is that the deal he was involved in putting together is not one that any CEO would orchestrate unless under pressure to do so. "I mean it was pretty onerous. I could understand if they basically said, 'we are not going to make a deal with you. We cannot negotiate a deal that satisfies us.' That would be fine. But the fact is that they did negotiate with us, and it did satisfy the staff, but the commissioners voted against it. It is something that will mystify me for the rest of my life."

Integrate with Caution

Integrate swiftly. We've heard this advice from many CEOs who have been involved in mergers, and we have given this advice as well (it's the title of a previous chapter, in fact). But wait just a minute, warns David Fuente, who would likely be joined by other CEOs who feel that they and their companies have been burned by the regulatory process.

"There is a tendency to want to move as quickly as possible to put the two companies together once a merger has been announced," says Fuente, describing what we have identified as a best practice. "And that typically means planning what the new organizational structure is going to be, including critical decisions about what people are going to be in key jobs, and so on.

"In the case of Office Depot and Staples, this was an inte-

The Human Side of M & A

gration project of enormous magnitude. Not only did we have the organizational issues, but we also dealt with issues of what stores were going to stay open, what stores were going to close. We had to address consolidating warehouses and as well as distribution systems internationally. We both had international agreements that we had to negotiate with our partners. The list goes on and on and on. So, it was an extremely complex integration process that I think was organized extremely well."

A company may not be able to recover from the human repercussions of a deal gone awry, says Fuente. People, and the critical roles they will play in the new organization, are at the core of how the business will operate going forward and will determine not only the effectiveness of the company but whether it will fulfill the promise of the merger. "When you say to somebody on the inside, 'You are not the chosen one for this job,' and the deal ultimately falls apart, resuscitating morale within the company and the self-esteem of individuals who were wounded in the process is a very difficult thing to do."

When the Office Depot–Staples deal went bust, Fuente completely changed his view of post-announcement, pre-approval integration. "I was always one of those fanatics who believed that when you conclude a deal, the next day, you should start the integration process so that when the deal closes you can essentially put the new organization in place on day one. And my attitude now is that if you are in a deal where there is any uncertainty about closing, a legitimate uncertainty about closing, I would not begin the integration process in a serious way. Obviously this has to be evaluated on a case-by-case basis, but I'd err on the side of caution. I might look at computers, I might look at some of the financial systems, but as far as integrating management teams, I'd wait."

Fuente is aware of the risk of not taking action to integrate—the uncertainty of doing nothing creates uncertainty and instability. But he says that if the outcome is not pretty well assured it is better to wait. Ultimately, is it better for people to live in a state of limbo or to be promised something that they are not going to get? "In my personal judgment," he says, "the answer is limbo."

Fuente had a couple of general suggestions concerning what might make the regulatory process run more smoothly. For one thing, he says, it would be more efficient if the Justice Department and the FTC worked through one regulatory agency instead of two. Moreover, he adds, the choice of consultants and counsel can also be critical: "I think the ideal would be to hire somebody to smooth the deal over and only bring in your litigator when you are actually litigating. In the final analysis, I would have been a little bit more cautious and probably hired a lawyer who was more politically astute."

A Matter of Balance

As David Fuente suggests, knowing what to expect during the regulatory process and responding appropriately and constructively are crucial to achieving the nod on a merger. And there are few people who understand the regulatory process as well as James Miller.

Miller was director of the Office of Management and Budget (OMB) under President Ronald Reagan and, prior to that, was chairman of the Federal Trade Commission. He has also taught on the university level and held a variety of positions in the private sector. For the first eight months of the Reagan administration, Miller was the executive director of the Presidential Task Force on Regulatory Relief headed by then vice president Bush. He was also an associate director at OMB. He now serves as chairman of the CapAnalysis Group, a consulting firm in Washington, D.C., associated with the law firm Howrey Simon Arnold & White.

"Our mission at OMB, as I helped to implement it as administrator, Office of Information and Regulatory Affairs, was to have a supervisory role over the executive branch regulatory function. In simplest terms, this not only gave some direction to regulatory agencies but held up a stop sign occasionally that told the agencies that they could not move forward because of insufficient predicate for their regulation or because they were adopting the wrong kind of regulation. In other words, under the executive order that President Reagan signed two weeks after taking office, the agencies had to prepare economic impact analyses for us to review and make a determination whether the predicate for the regulation made sense."

Though they may seem onerous to many companies, and perhaps senseless to others, there is a sound reason for most of the regulatory approval process that companies in many industries must go through in order to gain approval for a merger to proceed.

"There is a rationale for much of the regulation that we have," explains Miller, "especially in the health and safety areas, because we do not have property rights on certain parts of the environment, for example, the air we breathe and water in lakes and rivers. There are the 'third party effects' that economists talk about, and so the government steps in as a surrogate for property rights and has to apply some rules and regulations.

"In the so-called economic regulatory area," says Miller, "I think from left to right, from liberal to conservative, there is a general understanding that most of the cartel-type regulation, which was justified by the participants' own grounds of public interest, really doesn't make any sense. That's one reason we got rid of airline, trucking, and railroad regulation. But in the health, safety, and environmental areas, there is some justification for it."

Miller admits that government regulation in many industries, although necessary to protect citizens, is hardly a perfect science. Regulations can go too far or perhaps not far enough. It may be the wrong type of regulation to accomplish whatever the goal is or it may be an industry that the government has no business regulating in the first place. One point that Miller makes—a good one to keep in mind—is that in correcting one problem, the government can easily exacerbate the situation or create another problem. The government has imperfections of its own and regulation may sometimes entail merely overlaying one flawed process on another.

Competitive Advantages to Regulation

It is true, says Miller, that many companies view regulation as the price they have to pay for doing business, a thorn in their side. But the more savvy companies that really understand the process also understand that regulation can actually become an advantage to them when competitors may not be able to adapt as well to the regulatory environment. "Some companies feel very comfortable within the existing regulatory regime," says Miller, "because it reduces the threat from competitors who might come and take business away from them."

Further, explains Miller, there is a growing body of literature in economics indicating that companies can use the regulatory process to their advantage. They engage in what economists call "rent seeking" by encouraging the regulator to operate in a way that advantages them and disadvantages their competitors. There is a great deal of this activity in Washington.

"Let me give you one example," continues Miller. "When I was at the Federal Trade Commission, most of the new people were economists by training or had some economics background. We recognized very quickly what was happening when firms came in and would request a private conference to tell us what their competitors were doing. During my time at the FTC, this happened frequently. They would allege that their competitors were engaging in some unfair practice—false advertising, defrauding the public, or violating the Truth and Lending Act. They wanted to tip us off and encourage us to investigate their competitors."

By creating a disadvantageous situation for a competitor, a roadblock in the regulatory process that is something akin to being audited, companies were, in fact, deflecting scrutiny and creating an advantageous situation for themselves. That is rent seeking.

Frequently in the course of mergers and acquisitions, there is opposition from someone in the industry. Often, Miller says, this is an important signal to regulators. If a competitor objects that a merger will create a monopoly, chances are good that the deal will actually result in a supercompetitor. The real reason other companies in the industry object is that they fear the competition. When these deals are pending, there is a good deal of rent seeking by competitors. If they believe the merger will work to their advantage, they may support the merger, and if they think that the merger will work to their disadvantage, they may vehemently oppose it. While there may be other reasons for competitors speaking out, says Miller, "frequently you can tell whose ox is being gored by the one protesting the most."

Report Card

With the perspective of an outsider who has also worked on the inside when it comes to regulatory matters, Miller believes that overall the system works pretty well. He attributes much of the success to the sophistication of judges on economic matters, specifically in the area of mergers and acquisitions. Another reason it works well, he adds, is the evolution in thinking about antitrust that has occurred over the past three decades, which in his opinion has been for the better. "It is recognition," he says, "that bigness alone is not the same as monopoly power. It is a recognition that a number of activities that in the past were taken as evidence of monopolization are in fact evidence of competitive vigor."

Which is not to say that the regulatory process is perfect and cannot be improved. In Miller's view, key aspects of the process amount to roadblocks and should be modified. One is the sheer weight of the process. "Under the Hart Scott Rodino Act, even very small mergers can trigger filing requirements, delayed time periods in which you may not consummate the merger until you have a sign-off from the agency. The agency can continue to ask for additional information." Although the minimum trigger has been raised—which should alleviate some of the burden—he believes that complying with information requests is onerous and still tends to be unduly costly. Agencies could go through that a little faster and relieve some of the burden.

What regulators need to do, explains Miller, is measure the cost of any increase in these requirements for information against the barrier they create in deterring useful mergers or combinations. "Frequently, if you have a reasonably large merger, you are talking about boxes and boxes and boxes of responses to information that lawyers and officials of agencies have to go through. Tons of them—reams of reports, correspondences, and communications. They need to cull through the requests and separate out those they really need from those they do not. It is very burdensome and you need to make a call as to whether each additional increment generates some commensurate public good in terms of increasing the probability that you will detect a bad merger and what the public cost of such a bad merger might be."

The main problem is with the quantity of information needed to fulfill various requirements. The reasons for this are not difficult to understand. The lawyers in the Justice Department, Antitrust Division, for example, or the Federal Trade Commission, do not bear the cost of asking for too much information. But if they ask for too little and get caught later or find out that there was something they missed, that is a problem. So they have a tendency to ask for more than may be needed, to make sure they cover themselves.

"Similarly," observes Miller, "regulatory people at the FDA do not get into a great deal of trouble if they hold up a potentially useful new drug, but if they approve a new drug that turns out to be bad, then they really get hit."

It is natural that regulatory staff, who incur sanctions for not requesting enough information but not for requesting too much, will tend to err on the side of asking for too much information. Miller concludes that "in terms of the burdensomeness of the process and also the time in which the agencies have to review this material, both might be shortened. No draconian measures; it is not a matter of cutting it in half, but I think some fine-tuning there would make some sense."

As far as revisions in the actual regulations, Miller suggests following the advice given by the public policy group at the FTC and the chief economist office at the Antitrust Division. More checks are needed to ensure that the regulatory process does not become too onerous. For example, some kinds of information requests need to be approved by commissioners, not just FTC staff. In his previous life as an FTC commissioner Miller says he would require those asking for such information to justify exactly why it was necessary. Did they really think it would provide important additional details that could not be obtained elsewhere?

Timeliness is, of course, crucial in a merger, so any additional regulations that eat up time while the clock is ticking must be essential. "Bear in mind," says Miller, "that if a merger is truly justified and would increase competition and improve the value and resource allocation in the market, if you hold it up for a while, you lose those benefits during that period. Moreover, if you hold up a proposed merger that makes sense, if you erect barriers or threaten a proposed merger or acquisition, companies will be less interested in pursuing them and that too is an opportunity cost."

And word certainly gets around fast; companies contemplating mergers can be scared off by the painful experiences of others. Well-publicized cases in which people jump through hoops only to have the agency or the courts make a decision that appears arbitrary make others reluctant to invest time and energy in the same process and be faced with the prospect of achieving nothing. From a macro viewpoint, if the system discourages justified and pro-competitive mergers, it harms the allocation of resources in the market. Information request overkill can put the kibosh on individual mergers and cast a pall on the entire M&A environment.

The Rules of the Game

Individual tolerance, even for essential information requests, varies. "Some who understand how Washington works will understand the threat from Washington and do not want to make waves. Those who have been in Washington know how to make things work to their advantage," says Miller. "Take former Treasury Secretary Paul O'Neill, for example. He was deputy director of OMB in the Ford administration and later worked with a number of companies in the private sector. He is a guy who knows how Washington works and knows how to leverage that.

"On the other hand, I have encountered people who have very little knowledge of the ways of Washington and the threat that can be imposed on them. I remember sitting and hearing a presentation by the chairman of an oil company who was opposing a merger that we had before the Federal Trade Commission. He was there with his lawyer and I could just tell that the lawyer was a bit uncomfortable because his client was pretty outspoken. Finally, the fellow was rather exasperated that I did not get the point he was trying to make and he pounded the table and he said, 'Well, let me put it to you this way: I control the prices on the West Coast and those guys control them on the East Coast and I don't like it!' And I could see his lawyer ready to crawl under the table; his client was a real bull in a china shop. I suggested this man talk with his lawyer before saying anything more."

In one sense, the regulatory process is a game that has its own specific rules of compliance and decorum. It's a tough game and if you are going to get involved, you had better understand the rules and have all the appropriate experts at your disposal. And there is a cadre of people on L Street and K Street and Connecticut Avenue who make a lot of money guiding CEOs through the process, advising them on what to do and what not to do.

"I do not do this very often, but once I agreed to accompany a fellow down to the FTC to discuss a trade rule he was alleged to have violated. We were about to visit with some staff people at the FTC and I said, 'I hope we know each other well enough that you will take this in a constructive way. But before we go, take off that Rolex watch and take off the diamond stickpin, because you are going to be talking to people who do not make enough in a whole year to buy that diamond stickpin.'"

Room for Improvement

As someone well versed in M&A transactions in the highly regulated pharmaceutical industry, Glaxo SmithKline CEO J.-P. Garnier has suggestions on how the regulatory process can be improved. A native of Europe who has managed global operations, he also has had a good deal of experience with the European regulatory process there.

"The process should be realistic, pragmatic, and fast, whether in Europe or the U.S.," says Garnier. "It's certainly not fast, particularly in the U.S., and some of the rules are not adapted to today's reality."

One example Garnier points to is when a company has to make a disposal, which has to be accomplished before it enters into final negotiations and a consent agreement. "That is totally unrealistic and it forces companies to destroy value because it's a fire sale," says Garnier. "The Department of Justice in the U.S. should give us some time to sell, not a long time but six months perhaps. After all, what are the chances that we will turn around and say, 'Well, we're not doing it after all.' The enforcement powers of the Department of Justice are unlimited; there's no way a company would dare to do that.

"A regulation like this has negative repercussions for the

company and the shareholders, and frankly, it doesn't accomplish anything positive from the standpoint of competitiveness. When you have a fire sale you don't create the right set of circumstances."

The regulatory mind-set, observes Garnier, is quite different in Europe, where the general emphasis is on maintaining competitiveness, while in the U.S., the emphasis is on what is best for the consumer. Not mutually exclusive goals, but somewhat different priorities. They're looking at it through a different pair of glasses," says Garnier, "and companies have to adjust to that." He wonders (and worries) about the situation in a growing global regulatory environment in which each country involved in a multicountry merger might subject companies to similar competitive examination. "Today we have essentially Europe, the U.S., and Japan, but what if every country wanted to scrutinize mergers the way the U.S. does? What would happen? We would not have any transactions. So I think that big countries should be aware of the implications of potential overregulation; they should be pragmatic. They're exercising their right, but it should be done thoughtfully and purposefully so they don't create excessive bureaucratic and regulatory hurdles for companies that wish to merge." Garnier says he understands the philosophy underlying regulation and believes it is valuable, but he observes that sometimes the application is not as pragmatic as it might be considering the realities companies must deal with today.

As the regulatory process is drawn out, the impact on the business can be paralyzing. Garnier, like many experienced CEOs notes, "When you're in that period of having announced a merger but not yet able to unify the two companies, it's very difficult. And it creates distortions in the marketplace because you are immobilized; there are lots of things you suddenly can't do."

Planning in Limbo

Most CEOs we speak with, like Garnier, seem to understand the reasons for the regulatory process. But they find it very difficult to carry on with business as usual, plan for the proposed company's new future, and maintain morale and staff. Kent Foster is a veteran of the merger wars and seems to possess a balanced, calm view of the process, including of the limbo period.

CEO of Ingram Micro since 2000, Foster spent the previous twenty-nine years with GTE, where he was credited with helping lead the company from local telephone provider to global leader in telecommunications services. Before leaving the company, Foster was president of GTE telephone operations, responsible for the massive consolidation of fourteen autonomous operating companies into a single business unit. He was also a member of GTE's board of directors and a vice chairman.

"I think, honestly, in highly regulated industries or in situations where there are concerns at the Justice Department and other government agencies about the implications of a merger or an acquisition a longer process is entirely justified," says Foster. "Those mergers do take significant amounts of time because there are difficult issues for the regulators or the Justice Department to deal with."

Companies have gotten smart, says Foster, about finding ways to minimize the impact of the regulatory approval period on their existing teams by implementing a variety of retention techniques (see chapter 5). He acknowledges, for example, that the process GTE went through in merging with Bell Atlantic was a lengthy one, but does not believe that it had a dramatic negative impact on the companies' management teams. "That may not be what you expect to hear from me, but we kept things going, we kept things together by using various accepted retention techniques."

With these techniques available, Foster believes that the impact of this limbo period may be more deleterious for the business than the management teams. Dealing with the demands of various agencies does tie up senior management, he observes. "And since you have to work in lockstep with the merger partner or the company you are acquiring, it limits your flexibility. So, the business impact is more severe than the impact on the management team."

Acting speedily whenever possible, he says—in agreement with most of our other CEO sources—is crucial to the successful outcome of the merger, assuming it survives the regulatory process. "When you are putting together a merger," Foster says, "the first thing you want to do is start planning the new company. You don't want to lose time. Because even if takes a year or two to complete the deal, you want to be ready to hit the marketplace when the deal is approved."

One of the first steps in planning the new company is to announce the new management team. At this point the company is particularly vulnerable and will likely experience turnover. Here Foster advises caution. He argues in favor of holding off on announcing the new team as long as you can to avoid losing key people who may be vital if the deal is not consummated. "This delay, though, will cost you in terms of fully getting ready for the merger," he says. "You can have teams of people working together but until people know that there is someone in charge of a particular area, it's tough to make progress. It's more like a committee or a bureaucracy."

Deciding how and when to begin announcing the senior

executive team and begin mobilizing various functional areas is tricky, says Foster. "In everything you do, you're surrounded by devils. If you move too far one way, you have to deal with one devil, too far the other way another devil. So, what you want to do is operate as effectively as you can without moving too far in either direction."

That's difficult to do, of course, without naming the new leaders. But how do you know when is the right time? When is the merger enough of a definite go that the companies can risk naming one group of executives leaders at the risk of losing others? "I think you wait for certain signals or milestones," says Foster. "That might be waiting until you receive particular feedback from a regulatory agency so that you feel the probability of the deal going through is high. Whenever you reach a point where your confidence level is high, then you do it. Otherwise, I think you are taking extraordinary risks."

Weighing in on the Process

Overall, Foster expresses faith and confidence in the regulatory process and those who administer it. Nothing is ever 100 percent guaranteed, and things can always fall through, even after a series of positive signals; witness the outcome of the Office Depot–Staples deal. The only way to help ensure against such a disaster is for those who are involved in the regulatory process, on all sides, to be in regular communication so that they are aware of how things are proceeding and any problems that may be developing.

"My experience is that the various government agencies almost always act responsibly. These agencies have major responsibilities to carry out and represent important con-stituencies. They are thoughtful, intelligent, hardworking peo-ple. It's not a random process where you have wackos reaching ridiculous conclusions," says Foster reflecting on his own experience.

"At any point you can have an individual leader either on the business side or the regulatory side act inappropriately. But, by and large, that won't happen. If you step back and look at it from the perspective of the public, the agencies are playing an important role. We will obviously disagree and we can have strong convictions about our position, but that does not mean that either side is right or wrong."

An effective recourse Americans have, Foster points out, if the process seems to become capricious or irrational, is the courts. This avenue is not as useful in the European Commu-nity, he says, where it takes so long to navigate that it is not an effective mechanism to resolve a conflict in a merger and still have a chance of salvaging things. "But in the U.S. it's a very effective mechanism if you think a government agency is act-ing inappropriately or is not following the law. The courts will act and they will act quickly. So, the regulatory agencies and the Justice Department and businesses all have effective meas-ures to deal with inappropriate behavior."

Although the process calls for adjustments now and again, Foster believes it promotes what he deems the most advanced industries in the world. The adjustments are built in to the sys-tem. "What I've found in my career," he says, "is that if some-thing moves a little too far in one direction or the other, it will correct itself fairly quickly. The political process is self-healing and it will correct any mismoves fast. I think that that's a blessing that we have in this country. Not only do we have the checks and balances, but we have an overall political system that will effec-tively deal with anything that is out of line structurally."

Foster admits that we have too much regulation, though there has been a great deal of progress compared to twenty years ago. "But we need to do more. I think business should push back on government processes to make them as efficient and effective as possible."

Effective communications with regulators is one of the surest routes to success for a merger. Working with advisers who have been on the regulatory side is particularly helpful, not because they can lobby but because they understand the mind-set of those who will be requiring information and they understand the logic of the process. Getting the right information to the right people in a timely fashion is half the battle. And recognizing the responsibilities and mission of the regulators—which are totally different from what is motivating those on the business side—will help everyone get through the process more successfully.

Chapter 6 Planning Checklist

The period during which companies await regulatory approval for a merger can be a trying one for everyone, from the CEOs planning the transition to employees at all levels who await word of their fate. And, depending on the industry and the deal, this period can be a protracted one. Despite the frustration and uncertainty of waiting, however, there are a number of constructive steps companies can take to ensure that the new company, if given the green light, launches swiftly the day after the merger is consummated. Other steps help secure key employees and allow the company to maintain current operations and competitiveness during this limbo period. Following are some things to consider during this difficult time:

1. **There are no guarantees.** Any steps toward integration must be taken with caution, as the failed Office Depot–Staples merger highlights. There is never a guarantee of approval until it happens, and once certain integration steps are taken, and information shared, it's hard to go back.

2. **Wait on the press release.** Hold off on naming a new top management team until it is really safe to do so. Once executives learn they haven't made the cut, companies risk losing valuable talent if the merger is shot down by regulators.

3. **But don't wait too long.** The uncertainty and instability of not naming executive teams—and of people not knowing what their jobs will be and whom they will report to—creates its own set of problems. The key is timing. Don't announce the top management team if regulatory approval looks iffy, but don't delay announcing the team once regulatory approval appears likely.

4. **It's wise to incentivize.** Use incentives to help lock in key talent (specified in chapter 5) while the regulatory gears grind on.

5. **Seek good counsel.** Retain advisers who have been on the other side of the table, who understand the intent of regulations, the requirements to fulfill them, and how to work with regulators.

□   □   □

For mergers that are subject to regulatory approval, the process can exact quite a toll, on a human level as well as a business level. Those that survive intact can push ahead, but not without the right board to help guide the strategy and help

ensure fulfillment of the merger's goals. The next chapter provides specific recommendations on how companies can apply
some best practices and emerge with a board that will be a
valuable asset to the new company.

CHAPTER 7

Beef Up the Board

■

On the board level and on the management level there was
clearly an approach of inclusiveness, of picking the best that is
available and bringing those into Pfizer, and I think that was
done very well. By extending the olive branch, many of the bad
feelings that come with a hostile deal clearly were diffused and
were just not an issue anymore.

Alex Mandl, former Pfizer director
who also served on Warner-Lambert's board,
on Pfizer's merger with Warner-Lambert

Politically correct terminology and newspaper headlines
aside, mergers are virtually never "mergers of equals."
Whether companies and boards are joining forces in a merger
or an acquisition, in actuality one organization is always overtaking the other.

With governance increasingly in the spotlight, more companies, whether involved in a merger or not, will be paying
greater attention to getting their boards in line with key recommendations from the stock exchanges, as well as shareholder and government groups.

Immediately after the merger, CEOs may have less control
than they would like regarding the composition of their board.
Because of the public face they must present for one reason or
another, until they are over the hump of getting the merger
approved and on its feet, the combined company is often a case

of combining boards and the directors they comprise. This does not preclude planning beyond the initial period, however, and we advise boards to think ahead and actively shape the new board into one that reflects many of the best practices firmly associated with not only protection of shareholder interests but also the most successful companies.

In this chapter we first take a look at some of these corporate governance best practices, based on Spencer Stuart's ongoing research as well as our own consulting experience. We then examine what some companies are doing and what others can do to make the most of the opportunity, before and after a merger or acquisition, to get their board in shape.

A Constructive Approach

Particularly when it comes to a hostile takeover, where there doesn't have to be any public show of cooperation and equality, many acquiring companies do what may in the short run appear most efficient: displace the executives and directors of the acquired company with their own. As is often the case, however, the quick and easy solution may be shortsighted and militate against achieving longer-term objectives. Any company that wishes to boost morale as well as hold on to valuable management and board talent should carefully and systematically consider the resources in the company it is acquiring or merging with. Capable executives and directors are a valuable and scarce commodity; companies should think long and hard before cutting people loose for the sake of political expediency.

Pfizer acquired Warner-Lambert in 2000 in what was essentially a hostile takeover. As noted in chapter 4, Pfizer was clearly leading the merger process and was in a position to call the shots. But the CEO and his team recognized how important it was to the combined company's future and fulfilling the promise of the merger to establish and execute a fair process to evaluate and place executives in all key roles. They were determined to pick the "best of the best," as they put it—regardless of which side they were on—because they recognized this approach as the one from which the company and its shareholders would benefit.

Board Trends and Best Practices

For the past eighteen years, Spencer Stuart has published the Spencer Stuart Board Index (SSBI), a survey of the trends and practices of the boards of S&P 500 companies. Over time, we have observed some clear trends among these prominent, industry-leading companies that have become firmly associated with creating shareholder value.

We at Spencer Stuart have a long tradition of approaching corporate governance from a best practices point of view. There are practices undertaken by the boards of leading public companies with a long-term record of success and rewarding shareholders that we believe have become the standard of excellence for other companies to follow. These practices, some of which were considered a bit radical when we first began publishing the SSBI, now include commonly accepted tenets such as strictly limiting insiders on boards and prohibiting inside directors from serving on compensation and audit (and now governance) committees. Many of these model practices were intended—and not by accident—to strengthen directors' identification with the shareholders, whose interests they represent.

Fast-forward to the late 1990s and the giddy success of a pack of newly minted e-commerce companies. Many of these companies, observers noted (including us in our first report on Internet boards in 1999) defied much of the conventional wisdom on best practices but nonetheless achieved astounding gains for shareholders. "The old rules do not apply to this new and different upstart group," many said, and as long as these companies continued to produce great gains no one complained too loudly. But after the Internet sector crashed and burned several years ago, and especially since ensuing corporate scandals, attitudes about corporate governance and oversight have changed dramatically.

Now there is greater emphasis than ever on creating transparency in the boardroom, hiring capable directors, and adhering to corporate governance best practices. Finding and recruiting first-rate directors, however, is more difficult than ever before, for several reasons. First, boards are generally still getting smaller and recruiting directors is getting harder. The job has become more demanding, forcing executives—especially the traditional pool of board candidates, active CEOs—to be increasingly selective about directorships they are willing to take on.

Ironically, as fewer directors overall are being recruited and capable directors are more difficult to find, our board searches are up sharply. A contradiction? Not at all. Despite the constraints and added difficulties of recruiting directors, those who can contribute in the boardroom are a vital resource, now more than ever. Our clients recognize this fact and realize they need every advantage they can muster in attracting the best directors for their boards.

Golden Opportunity

In view of the difficulty of recruiting directors in today's business climate, companies should seize the opportunity to enhance their board with talented senior executives on the boards of companies they may be acquiring or merging with. A merger is also an ideal time to generally take stock of the ongoing board's composition and practices and, to the extent possible, align the board with what are considered progressive and productive corporate governance guidelines.

The following profile is gleaned from our 2003 annual board survey as well as from practices of the most successful companies we work with:

- Boards are getting smaller. For the eighteen years we have been publishing the SSBI, one of the most consistent trends has been the paring down of boards. Some ten years ago the average board in our survey comprised fourteen directors. By today's standards that's large. The average S&P 500 board in 2003, according to our survey, had eleven directors. The impetus for smaller boards may be slightly different now. Earlier, the trend was more likely a result of boards intentionally slimming down, particularly by reducing the number of inside executives, to operate more efficiently and effectively. Today, it may say more about the difficulty of replacing directors when they depart.
- Committees are more important. The number of standing committees maintained by boards has plateaued at four for the S&P 500. Though boards have shrunk substantially in recent years, the average number of committees has remained the same, indicating that remaining board members are more actively involved on committees and that a greater proportion of the board's work is being done by committees.
- Fewer CEOs now are also chairmen. While traditionally

CEOs in the United States have also been chairmen of their boards, currently only three-quarters of S&P 500 CEOs hold both titles, and it appears the number may be decreasing. Splitting the chairman and CEO roles is often a transitional phase for a company. The former CEO may remain on the board for a bit while the new CEO gets his or her footing, or a founder or major shareholder may want continued representation. Alternatively, it may reflect a tumultuous period at a particular company or may be the result of a merger agreement.

- There is far greater board independence. For years we (and others who advocate best practices) have stressed the importance of board independence, a topic that has recently seized everyone's attention. Nowhere is this principle more critical than on the audit and compensation committees, two areas that present the greatest potential for conflict of interest and other difficulties if not properly overseen. While 100 percent independence (i.e., only outside directors) is particularly crucial on the audit committee, at least a couple of S&P 500 boards have not yet hit the mark. As we found in our 2003 report, 98 percent of S&P 500 boards' audit committees overall are independent, and 96 percent of compensation committees. In the case of other committees, independence depends on the specific mandate of the committee and whether it is better carried out by a majority of outsiders.

- Boards are coming into compliance with now required board evaluations. When asked if their board has a formal board evaluation process, 87 percent of respondents indicated that they evaluate the entire board's performance, as opposed to 38 percent that evaluate individual director performance (not required).

Constraints in Establishing Postmerger Boards

Often the composition of the emerging company's board is spelled out in the merger agreement. That does not mean, however, that a great deal of thought is given to getting the most capable directors on the board; it may be strictly a game of ratios and formulas.

"Boards after mergers, especially if it is a merger of roughly equivalent firms, often reflect the merger but poorly represent the shareholder," says Wharton School management professor Michael Useem. "They draw large numbers of directors from both companies, frequently resulting in what amounts to two amalgamated boards that are far from meeting the contemporary standards of good governance."

Part of the problem is the challenge of size and integration: "The result," says Useem, "is that the boards can be very unwieldy. If it is a matter of taking both boards and simply joining them at the hip, the product is a large number of directors who have no shared culture or common history. While the new board may reflect the personal reality of what it took for each side to approve the merger, the result is a governing body less than ideal for making the deal work after the merger.

"In the U.S., boards normally have anywhere from ten to fifteen members," explains Useem. "When boards become much larger than that, research studies indicate that their performance tapers off. Thus, big is bad when it comes to American boards. If the two partners each appointed most or all of their premerger directors to the new board, we may now see a board with twenty or even thirty directors, a size that will not be optimal in the long run or even near term. If the merged firms are operating in a fast-moving industry, a board with a score or more directors is unlikely to have the capacity to make the rapid decisions required."

Like Useem, we believe that assembling the board that will guide the merged companies requires as much thought and planning as the merger itself. And the more discussion and planning ahead of time the better. Putting the board together is not something that should be accomplished as an after-thought in a last-minute effort to ensure that the deal goes through. As Useem sums up, "The board and its operations in a postmerger era—its mission, size, principles, and policies—have to be part of a formula that is pursued in advance of the close." And it's the CEO's job to ensure that this is done prop-erly. The merger team in a company that is experienced and proficient at making these deals happen can handle much of the integration mechanics, but the board is a step above the level at which the merger team is operating and so must be negotiated by the CEOs.

Back to Basics When Building the Board

Steve Kaufman is the recently retired chairman and CEO of Arrow Electronics, the $10 billion global distributor of semi-conductors and computer products and senior lecturer of business administration for Harvard Business School. The company grew from $300 million in sales in 1982 to $10 billion in 1991. Kaufman has completed sixty acquisitions over the past twenty years, twenty in the United States, and forty in Europe and Asia. All of the M&A activity has been in Arrow's own industry (i.e., buying competitors or expanding into new geographies by acquiring a leading company in that country).

Given his significant experience in the M&A realm, Kauf-man is quite familiar with the formulaic approach to building the combined company board. The board A plus board B equals board C equation is often a necessary step to get over the threshold of merger approval, even if it is not the ideal board to live with indefinitely. It may be a purely transitional one.

"Reconfiguring a board after a transaction entails a lot of sticky political problems," says Kaufman. "Very often the most difficult situation is in what is called a 'merger of equals,' which actually only exists in the fictional minds of business writers. Many of these mergers are predicated upon a reasonable combination and that means that there are implicit or explicit promises made about the configuration of the board. If it is going to be split fifty-fifty, it is going to be five of yours, and five of mine; or six of mine and five of yours. Or it's a formula based on the exchange of shares. There are often commitments made and those commitments are hard to work out. Sometimes they are made because the acquired company wants some leverage, some assurance that promises are going to be kept. They are really putting board members on to make sure that the deal is coming along the way it is supposed to."

Like Useem, Kaufman points out that these critical decisions are frequently made in a period of pressure near the end of the negotiation when most of the business issues are completed and the "social issues," as they are referred to, are being considered. And they are often made without a lot of thought.

"So when CEOs say, 'all right, all right, you can have three more members,' people do not think through the implications of that; they are so anxious to get to the finish line. They are not considering the problems they may set up in terms of having to cycle unneeded or unwanted directors off the board in the future."

Another set of difficult circumstances, says Kaufman, can arise in connection with a pure cash deal, when the CEO of the acquired company is offered a seat as a gesture of respect and continuity, even if he is retiring or not continuing in the business. "They figure the selling CEO will want to have something to do during the next year or two so he does not have to leave cold turkey," exclaims Kaufman. "And that becomes sticky as well because there have not been explicit discussions about how long, and what roles, and under what circumstances do we conclude that this relationship is not working."

What does Kaufman suggest when determining the most effective composition of a postmerger board? "You set up a straw dog" (which he says is the politically correct term for straw man). "What do you want your board to be? Whether it is a merger or a new CEO coming into an interim situation, or a new CEO coming in under a succession program, you go back to fundamentals. My basic rules are: number one, eliminate certain classes of people that should never be directors.

"On the boards of public companies, for-profit organizations, I believe that rule includes not having practicing lawyers, investment bankers, and commercial bankers on the board. Except perhaps in the case of an LBO of a private company where you may need to have private equity investors on the board, I do not believe that you should ever have on the board individuals whose current professional activities include giving advice or selling services to similar companies."

Accountants, says Kaufman, also fall into this group but have to follow professional guidelines prohibiting them from sitting on boards. He also includes management consultants. "If you had a person on your board from one of those organizations, you have two problems. When you go to select a firm to provide those services to the corporation, you have either an explicit conflict or an awkwardness about who is picked or not picked. Secondly, either from the service that those companies provide or from the people inside the company who practice in that arena, you wind up with the possibility of disagreement on the board. For example, you have a lawyer from a big-name law firm on your board. You have an issue and your general counsel or the external law firm you are using opines, here is the issue and here is what we should do.

"You may well get conflicting advice from two professionals and inevitably, most professionals in a board situation tend to reach and seem more expert in that particular area than they actually may be. So you may have a securities lawyer on the board and, even if it is a labor law issue, the securities lawyer may still get into a fight with the general counsel. He will have an opinion whether he knows something or not. Rarely correct, but never in doubt.

"So, rule number one: People who would provide services for the firm should never be on the board. And I would make it an absolute, ironclad rule so that you never have a problem: 'Oh, he was a really good guy, he has been on the board for years,' yadda, yadda, yadda. That is where you run into problems as they age or get away from active practice."

The issue can become particularly ugly with investment bankers and commercial bankers, says Kaufman, because they are wholly out there for transactions and dollars. And they will get into "pissing contests" with the outside professionals you hire. "When you need great professional services, go out and hire the very best and pay them at top dollar. Do not try to get that kind of professional service on the cheap by having a $100,000-a-year board member."

Maintaining ironclad rules about who may and may not serve as a director helps get around some of the sticky issues that arise when companies merge. "If you lay down that first rule, when you look at the eleven on my team and the ten on your team, maybe four can be eliminated just like that. 'Oh, he is really great,' one CEO may say about a particular board member. Then let us hire him as a consultant," suggests Kaufman.

The second rule, according to Kaufman, is that you have to have an age limit and you have to enforce it, even if it is painful. This must hold true even if it means that a young seventy- or seventy-two-year-old director may have to go off the board, just because once you start making waivers, particularly after you accept this rule, you have a precedent. After you have adhered to the policy a few times, he says, you can then have a specific waiver for one or two years, perhaps for reasons of continuity. Enforcing this rule enables boards that could be too large as a result of a merger to whittle down in size by focusing on the oldest members who will have to give up their directorships soon.

"If you are very Machiavellian, you might deliberately leave a seventy-year-old or two on the board so that the issue does not have to be addressed now. That way some other people whom you would rather not have on the board would get squeezed out while the seventy-year-old will have to retire from the board soon anyway. So if you look at the cast of characters and you are negotiating the decision, maybe you will pick a distinguished seventy-one-year-old to avoid a fifty-five-year-old who you sense would not be constructive on the board going forward."

In addition to the guidelines already mentioned, Kaufman does not believe it is wise to have directors from narrowly drawn constituencies. Directors should represent all shareholders, he insists, not a narrow slice of them. "That is why I do not like the lead director concept because that is saying that some directors are more equal than others. All directors have to focus on the long-term good of the whole company."

Finally, and importantly, says Kaufman, is the critical objective of building a board whose members will be able to contribute to the substantive discussions of the issues, strategies, and environments that the company operates in.

It is important, he emphasizes, to have directors whose personal backgrounds, and personal career development, have been in the key functions for this business. "As an electronics distributor, one of the two or three most critical functions for us is sales. I quickly decided it was crucial that I have one or two board members whose personal careers were in industrial sales so that I could have help and counsel in tackling key sales-oriented issues, such as motivating a sales force. I also like to have one or two board members who have had careers closely associated with finance. They are important resources when dealing with issues such as getting capital, debt versus equity, and how to evaluate investment bankers. It's also important to have someone on the board who came up the operations route and is familiar with all the day-to-day challenges we deal with."

Whether planning for a postmerger board or any other board, Kaufman says it comes down to "Okay, who do I want on my board? I want at least a couple of practicing, active CEOs and COOs. I want a couple of people in functions that are critical to our business. So you make up a spec sheet. Those are the things I suggest anyone do anytime they are building a board."

Look in Your Own Backyard

Going back to basics—solid recruiting tenets—is always a good idea when building a board. And companies should not overlook capable directors who may be right under their nose. Just as we advise companies involved in mergers or acquisitions to carefully assess talent on both sides before deciding on whom to place where on the new team, similarly, companies should carefully size up director talent. In an environment where director talent is increasingly difficult to attract, don't automatically eschew capable directors on the board of a target company for an acquisition or merger. They can prove to be a valuable, available resource that may be a great asset to the new board.

In the case of the 2000 Pfizer acquisition of Warner-Lambert, Pfizer acted wisely in a situation that was essentially a hostile takeover where Pfizer was in no way beholden to the Warner-Lambert board. Pfizer recognized the difficulty of recruiting director talent and looked to the acquisition.

"They picked up several of us, actually," says Alex J. Mandl, CEO of Paris-based Gemplus International SA, the world's leading provider of smart card solutions and former Warner-Lambert director. Because he is now based in Europe, Mandl had to resign from the Pfizer board. But he recalls how skillfully Pfizer's CEO at the time of the acquisition of Warner-Lambert, William C. Steere, Jr., currently chairman emeritus, diffused a potentially awkward board situation with his statesmanlike approach. "I don't know what was in Bill's or Hank's (McKinnel, Steere's successor and the current Pfizer CEO) mind, but I think it was principally a way of neutralizing the hostile environment. And I think the whole concept of diffusing the situation went well beyond just the board. It extended to offers to many key Warner-Lambert people."

Including Warner-Lambert directors on the new board was more than a symbolic gesture because it added great value to the new board and the new company. "I think they strengthened their own board and provided some new perspectives," reflects Mandl. "And it certainly gave Warner-Lambert board members the assurance that they would be there to see that whatever promises were made were being kept." It did not develop into an "us versus them" board, however. "Very quickly, the board integrated and became a cohesive well-functioning unit."

As many who know Bill Steere have observed, he personally pulled the new board together in a way that is unusual for CEOs. "He called everyone on Warner-Lambert's board and invited us to come in and to speak with him, to extend the offer personally and to discuss what was on our mind." While not everyone accepted the offer—including some who were close to retirement—Steere's approach helped the combined companies get off to a promising start.

Like Pfizer, Rohm & Haas—the Philadelphia-based specialty materials company—also looked to the board of an acquisition for director talent to help augment its own resources. Nineteen ninety-nine was a big year for the company. In addition to a planned change in CEOs (current CEO Rajiv Gupta succeeded J. Lawrence Wilson) the company made three acquisitions that doubled its size, from $3.5 billion to $7 billion.

"Very early in the game," says Gupta, "we knew that each of the three transactions was an acquisition by Rohm & Haas, so there was no illusion that it was a merger of equals." Though Rohm & Haas was under no formal obligation to add anyone from the acquired company to its board, the CEO decided it was the smart thing to do, especially given the size of the Morton acquisition, the largest of the three, and the desire to ensure its success.

In addition to the CEO transition, Rohm & Haas was facing attrition on its board as some directors approached the mandatory retirement age of seventy. "Out of thirteen board members, we had two insiders, a CEO and a COO, who were retiring. We have what we believe is a great policy of not having ex-executives on the board. And we only have a maximum of two insiders on the board. In addition to the holes left by the CEO and COO, a handful of other directors would be retiring, so effectively we were shrinking down by about 50 percent during about a year and a half," explains Gupta. The new CEO, Gupta, and the new COO, J. Michael Fitzpatrick, would be added to the board, as well as two Haas family members. Although there was no commitment to bring anyone from the two smaller acquisitions on the board, it was important to integrate Morton into the board.

"Morton senior management was going to retire fairly imminently," explains Gupta, "and we felt it would be worthwhile for us to bring on at least a couple of directors from Morton to continue to give some perspective on the company's history. The CEO of Morton suggested a couple of outstanding candidates from their board and both of them have made excellent additions to the board. They not only provided valuable insight into Morton's history and businesses and now, a few years later, they have also proven excellent long-term board members."

Overall, Gupta is quite satisfied with the board he actively helped assemble after recent attrition and the merger with Morton. "I have been very happy with the way the board functions at Rohm & Haas," he says. "They are engaged, interested, supportive, and ask the right questions. They play a crucial role." They also help keep the CEO on his toes: "I am regularly reviewed by my directors, and this is a serious review. I am accountable to my fourteen bosses."

Hilton and Promus: Guidance from a Strategic Acquisition

When a company makes a strategic foray into a new or related business, moving directors from the acquired company on to the board is often a smart move. Hilton Hotels president and CEO Stephen F. Bollenbach decided to do this when Hilton acquired Promus in November 1999. In every sense, says Bollenbach, the acquisition of Promus—about 40 percent the size of Hilton—was a strategic one. While Promus was also in the hotel business, their emphasis was on franchising, something Hilton had a great interest in pursuing more aggressively than it had before. "They owned some hotels and managed others, as we do," says Bollenbach, "but the focus was on franchising their brand."

The directors on Promus's board would provide a critical link in helping Hilton's CEO and board make the right decisions in broadening Hilton's business opportunities with greater franchising. Unlike what is often the case with acquisitions, this was not an instance of a company entering a new business and reaching out to board members of the acquired company to gain skills and understanding of the industry that might be lacking on the acquirer's board. Here the focus was interest in maintaining continuity of knowledge about the acquired company to ensure that that the strategic reason for the acquisition was fully realized.

"We had an opportunity to attract two really outstanding board members from Promus's board," says Bollenbach, "and we jumped at the opportunity. We were successful in recruiting Peter Ueberroth, managing director of the Contrarian Group and cochairman of Pebble Beach Company, and John Myers, who is president and CEO of General Electric Asset Management. Both are very experienced and capable directors. And it was the only way we could have attracted John Myers; General Electric does not generally allow their executives to serve on outside boards but made an exception in the case of Promus."

The acquisition, says Bollenbach, has been a perfect combination of the companies' management with none of the integration problems he views as so typical of acquisitions or mergers. The new directors, he adds, have been a key factor in the successful integration as well as important contributors to the combined board as a whole. "And if not for the acquisition, we would probably never have had the opportunity to recruit them. Obviously, we could not have recruited them when they were on the board of a competitor. Even if for some reason they had left Promus's board, we couldn't have gotten either one. General Electric would not have encouraged John Myers to join and Peter Ueberroth would have been too much in demand by other boards."

Bollenbach and other CEOs we spoke with evidently appreciate the fact that it is increasingly difficult to recruit capable directors. Attracting them, suggest Bollenbach, is a matter of their level of interest in a particular company combined with available time to put in the necessary work rather than compensation that is offered. "I know it sounds kind of elitist in a country where average board fees sound like a lot of money to most people, but most directors I know do not do it for the money; it is not what attracts them to serving on a particular board. Board fees are sort of irrelevant."

Bollenbach believes that Hilton has been very fortunate in the directors it has attracted, including those from the Promus acquisition. "They provided a history and continuity with the old business. From a management perspective, we had plenty of opportunity to study and understand the business during the period of our due diligence. But I found it very helpful that there were people who could help educate us, board member to board member, on the way in which their business worked relative to ours—specifically in the franchise business, which was the core of what we acquired. It is not a business in which you measure success in returns on assets because there is not much in the way of assets in a franchise business; you need to measure it in terms of your ability to expand the system and make the system valuable to the franchisees. It is the hotel business but it is a really different slant on how you measure success, and I think that it is very helpful to have people who have been doing that for a long period of time in their prior company."

While Hilton benefited greatly from the addition of the two former Promus directors, Bollenbach firmly believes that it is unwise to "bake" into the acquisition or the merger agreement requirements to take on specific board members. "You want to avoid conflict at the board level as much as possible and, in the context of mergers and acquisitions, you want to think about the board as an opportunity to attract people you might not otherwise be able to get. And to the extent you can, you really want to avoid rigid requirements to take on certain directors, which adds another major element of risk."

Chapter 7 Planning Checklist

From the standpoint of corporate governance best practices, mergers present a rare opportunity for boards to really shape up. Here are some tips to keep in mind.

1. **Seize opportunity.** Recognize that capable directors are a scarce commodity and use a merger or an acquisition as an opportunity to recruit them.
2. **Raise the bar.** Be aware of generally accepted corporate governance practices, which correlate with good company performance, and consider bringing your board into line where gaps exist.

3. **Resist simple math.** Try to steer clear of the "one from our side one from yours" formula when establishing a post-merger board, or you may be left with a legacy of underperforming directors.

4. **Put skills first.** Carefully consider the skills and experience you will need on the board and select directors accordingly.

5. **Exploit an overlooked resource.** Particularly in an acquisition, where there may be no obligation to take on directors, carefully assess talent and opportunity on the board of the acquired company.

☐   ☐   ☐

Mergers and acquisitions present a number of opportunities to build a better board that will not only help the company during the deal but will also serve as a resource going forward. Implementing board best practices is a critical step to getting a company on solid footing after a merger or an acquisition. The following chapter summarizes all of our recommended best practices.

CHAPTER 8

Conclusion
The Lucky Seven: Best Practices
for Successful Mergers

■

L ike other economic phenomena, M&A activity comes in
clearly defined waves. The wave that peaked in 2000 has
been well documented. And despite the retrenchment overall
in the economy over the last few years—including in the merger and acquisition climate—we can expect to see M&A activity rebound in the coming years.

Why is that? Because M&A is not a passing fancy; em-
ployed properly it is an enduring strategy. The reasons it is
used as part of a strategy are many and may include:

- Acquiring talent, whether management or more specific
  expertise
- Building reputation in the marketplace
- Reducing operating expenses or costs
- Acquiring new products
- Increasing market share in current or complementary business
- Having rapid access to new markets or new industry
- Reducing the number of competitors
- Gaining access to new technology, manufacturing capacity,
  or suppliers

While there may be peaks and valleys, the perennial reasons for mergers remain. Whether merger activity is at a

high or low ebb, there is no arguing with the facts. Synergies are eagerly anticipated but often the results, after all the numbers are run and agreements signed, range from disappointing to downright dismal. The key variable that separates the successes from the failures—as we have argued throughout this book—is the human factor: before, during, and after the deal. Mistakes that may inflict serious damage to fulfilling the vision of the merger, or may even lead to its demise, range from errors in judgment made early on, such as attempting to merge two companies that are hopelessly at odds with each other culturally, to not taking the right steps later on to ensure the company retains the talent needed to make the merger work.

While companies don't always do the soul-searching or the planning required for success in this realm, the good news is that much can be done, during each phase and at every organizational level, to help secure an optimal outcome. We are not suggesting that merger planning and integration is a perfect science; far from it. But with a good deal of thought beforehand and diligent planning and follow-through afterward, companies can greatly increase their chances of success and avoid a drain on both human and financial resources.

With just that sort of planning and follow-through in mind, in the remainder of this chapter we have distilled the main theme of each preceding chapter in this book down to a best practice.

Improve the Odds

It doesn't take a business historian to grasp the lessons from failed mergers of the past. Even a cursory analysis of many of the high-profile mergers that were either abandoned or proved less than successful demonstrates that a lack of consideration for the human factor—the softer cultural elements that cannot be viewed on spreadsheets—is a surefire formula for disaster. We have all read the news stories: attention-grabbing headlines followed in short succession by a postmortem of what went wrong. And all too often the merger's demise is traced back to an almost exclusive focus on the numbers or to the blinding exuberance of CEOs who focused so narrowly on the promise of the merger that they glossed over the many intricate steps it would take to get there.

When we suggest in chapter 1 that companies improve their odds of success, we mean that they should not only heed the lessons of mergers past but also be realistic and practical about all the work it will take to achieve the goals of the merger. In addition, they should be aware of the many substantial obstacles to integration when merging two cultures, obstacles that are not necessarily insurmountable but should not be underestimated. Here too, the lessons of the past (the successful lessons, that is) are instructive, and we've tried to provide positive examples of companies that have prevailed by following best practices.

Take Stock of Human Capital

Human talent and leadership are at the very crux of what makes some mergers and acquisitions successful and others not. Too often, particularly in an acquisition where companies are not obligated to consider managers outside their own organization, valuable talent is overlooked. In the confusion of integration, unless there is a solid and objective assessment process in place, decision makers may easily lose sight of what made the acquisition an attractive target in the first place. Very often, a primary attraction is management talent. Great products and services don't develop and sell themselves, and the people behind these successes must be systematically identified and assessed for fit in the new company. The key baseline comparison for all of these evaluations is the overall vision and strategy of the new company going forward. The new leadership must include those who are capable managers in their own right and also have the right skills and experience to propel that strategy.

Self-serving though it may sound, since management evaluations represent a major business segment for us, it is wise to have an objective third party undertake these assessments. This levels the playing field by dispensing with any preconceived notions about the pluses and minuses of individual executives, and the entire process is more easily embraced by all as being fair and equitable. The results, whether perceived as good or bad by any one individual, have greater credibility across both organizations.

Most merger-tested CEOs we spoke with recommend beginning the evaluation and integration process as soon as the merger is announced so that, when it is finally approved, the new organization will be ready to roll from day one. Others recommend caution. There can sometimes be unpleasant surprises, and once two companies share competitive secrets and make key decisions about what the management team will look like (and who will go), it may be impossible to recover if the merger does not go ahead.

Create a New Vision

The culture that emerges from a merger ideally should not represent the legacy of either individual company but should be compatible with the vision and goals of the new company. It should look to the future and what it hopes to accomplish, not the past.

Defining the vision, as well as the culture in which it will be realized in day-to-day, operational terms, is a complex, multi-layered process. Critical decisions must be made about the more obvious elements that comprise the personality of a company, including decision making, compensation, metrics, and systems. But less obvious idiosyncratic elements, such as dress, behavior, and communication, are also key and can prove to be stumbling blocks that may lead to a company's downfall. All of these elements must somehow be defined and communicated in the effort to create one company with one prevailing culture.

Above all, say those who have been through the postmerger integration process, clarity of goals and speed of decision making are key to a good outcome. Managers in the new organization want to build a success, but they need to know precisely what the new rules are, how that success will be measured, and what is expected of them in their individual roles.

Nothing is more essential to aligning the culture with the new vision than having the right talent in place to execute the strategy. Integration after a merger is an uncertain and unnerving time for managers; their routine and expectations have been disrupted, and they may not yet know what will replace them. That is why it is so important to identify, court, and retain the talent that will be critical to realizing the dream of the merger.

No matter where individuals come from—either company or the outside—acculturation is an important aspect of integration after the merger. Many companies have structured orientation programs that equip managers with the skills and even the vocabulary they will need to succeed in their new positions in the new organization.

Retain and Motivate Key Players

A central thesis of this book is also a statement that cannot be repeated too often in the context of mergers and acquisitions: The right management team is so critical to making the deal work that leaders must identify these players early on and do everything reasonably possible to retain them.

Executives who will be needed going forward are not always the most obvious or most vocal individuals, which means that you need to do a careful, objective assessment of both management teams before making decisions about who belongs in what position. The transition period in which all these decisions and changes are made is exceedingly stressful for those who remain and those who leave. Every effort must be made to maintain an orderly, rational process and to communicate changing roles and responsibilities as soon as possible. Reaffirming the business case for the merger and identifying those who will be important in executing the strategy will help determine who the keepers will be.

Once the company has determined those it will make efforts to retain, there are a variety of retention vehicles to consider. The tools to be applied—and the expense—will depend on how integral the individual will be to the new regime. Retention may be viewed as short- or long-term, strictly to get over the hump of the merger or, alternatively, to help execute the strategy. Compensation is not the only variable involved in holding on to people. Quality-of-life issues, both personal and company-related, can be important considerations when people decide whether to remain with a company or to leave.

What will the impact be on their family? Is the culture and reputation of the company one they are comfortable with? These kinds of important factors will affect decisions to stay or to perhaps explore other opportunities.

Integrate Deliberately and Swiftly

Assuming the reasons and the foundation for the merger are solid, speed is a critical component of the equation for success. All of the integration activity that must be addressed in a merger—a myriad of cultural, systems, and compensation elements—must be accomplished efficiently if the new company is to hit the ground running and retain key people in the process. To speed integration, CEOs and human resources specialists recommend driving the mission of the merger home through frequent and consistent communications and forums at all levels. The mission should be boiled down to something simple and to the point. One merger veteran suggested that it should fit on the back of a business card.

The direct involvement and judgment of CEOs is indispensable during the integration process, no matter what size army they have at their disposal. Charismatic, action-oriented CEOs send a strong signal from the top about the company's mission and vision. While it will be up to others at every level to help employees understand, in operational terms, the roles they will play, the CEO can help pull the disparate groups together and put people at ease.

One of the most critical decisions to make early on is precisely what the management team will look like. Leadership at every level must be clarified as quickly as possible. Appointing coheads in any area leads to confusion and frustration and is best avoided. If absolutely necessary, there should be clear ground rules defining responsibilities as well as the time frame for any shared positions.

Survive the Regulatory Process

Companies that require regulatory approval, which can be time-consuming and occasionally unpredictable, must take some care during the limbo period (after the merger is announced but before it gets the regulatory nod). Key decisions about choices for leadership positions, once announced, are difficult to take back. If for some reason the merger is killed, trust and confidence can be difficult if not impossible to repair, and those who were told they would be let go will likely seek opportunities elsewhere. CEOs who have been burned by the regulatory process are particularly wary, preferring to live in uncertainty—and with whatever negative repercussions for morale—than to jump the gun and make announcements they may later regret.

Most of the CEOs we spoke with, though in regulated industries, had surprisingly few negative comments about the regulatory process. They understand its crucial protective role for citizens and consumers and do not view it as unbearably onerous. Can things be improved? Of course, they say, but it's more tinkering that is required than a complete overhaul.

One issue regarding regulation that may become more of a factor in the future is when the requirements of one regulatory process potentially pile on top of another in global mergers. There is a balance that needs to be maintained: protecting the interests of society at large while not inhibiting more efficient and beneficial business combinations.

Experienced CEOs and former regulators we spoke with offer one piece of advice: Hire attorneys and other advisers who know the regulatory process, are respected by those in regulatory agencies, and understand what will be expected of the company. Those who were once on the regulatory side can be especially helpful because they are more likely to understand the mind-set and what will be required to gain approval.

Beef Up the Board

From the point of view of building a formidable board—both adding and replacing directors and implementing best practices—a merger or acquisition can present a rare opportunity.

When planning changes to the board, it is important to keep a couple of factors in mind:

- Because of increased responsibilities "at home" on boards, traditionally in-demand directors (i.e., CEOs) are far tougher to recruit.
- You may have to live with any additions to the board for a long time, even if changes are politically motivated and intended merely to get the deal done.

The smart companies are those that look at a merger as a chance to make a fresh start: whether the goal is building greater independence into the board or adding new skills that will help the company fulfill the new vision. That might mean adding a non-U.S. director who will help open a new market, adding needed financial or technical expertise, or perhaps diversity that will enhance understanding of the needs of critical customer populations.

Because recruiting capable directors is difficult, companies should look to acquisitions as a good source of talent for their board. The desire on both sides to build institutional memory of the acquisition into the deal and help things get off to a smooth start may mean that sought-after directors who would not normally be available to serve on a board are available to move to the acquirer's board. They can provide invaluable guidance as one company is folded into another.

Although it is a common tactic, companies should resist the shortsighted, clumsy, often ineffective approach of simply throwing the boards of both companies in a merger to create one big, bloated board. Better to properly plan, well ahead of time, for the board that will best help fulfill the vision of the merger than to take the path of least resistance early on and then be saddled with the consequences. Planning against a matrix of best governance practices as well as a company's specific strategic goals is still the best way to shape up a board—merger or no merger.

□   □   □

Given the many reasons that M&A may prove to be an effective part of a company's long-term strategy—and given that the reasons are inherent to success in a free market economy—we are confident mergers will remain a staple of economic activity, albeit one that occurs in definable waves. Executed with care and attention to the all-important human and cultural elements, not just spreadsheets, mergers and acquisitions can produce great benefits in terms of growth, cost-cutting, R&D, opening new markets, and not incidentally for shareholders. With a great deal of planning, and some luck, M&A will continue to be a fruitful path for many companies. With eyes wide open to not only the best practices we have delineated but also the pitfalls, we hope to help greatly increase the chances for success.

Smart Money and Smart Bidders

Sanjai Bhagat, Professor of Finance

University of Colorado at Boulder

The following research was undertaken by Spencer Stuart in June 2002 to identify the most successful mergers from 1990 to 2002 as defined by return to shareholders. Not coincidentally, the companies that employ best practices regarding human capital—such as identifying key talent, integrating swiftly, and rewarding key players—fall within this high-achieving group. The authors believed that this analysis would be of interest to readers and would provide a broader context in which to view the largest, most successful mergers.

Mergers and takeovers are ubiquitous in both the corporate and the economic landscape of the free world. During 1999, there were more than 8,000 merger announcements (an all-time high) in the United States alone. The dollar value of the announced merger transactions involving U.S. targets during 1980–2002 is over $12 trillion. Given the frequency and dollar value of such transactions, one might logically ask, Why do bidders bid? Perhaps the bidding managers are able to redeploy the target's assets to create a whole that is greater than the sum of its parts. If that is the case, then mergers should increase the wealth of bidding shareholders.

A substantial number of academic papers have attempted to measure the wealth impact of mergers on bidding and target shareholders (see Bhagat, Hirshleifer, and Noah, 2002, for a recent example of such research). There is strong consensus in the academic literature that target shareholders experience a significant positive wealth effect of 30–50 percent. There is also strong consensus in the academic literature that, on average, bidding shareholders do not experience any significant wealth effect on announcement of such mergers. Depending on the sample period and sample considered, studies document average bidder returns that cover the range from positive, economically small, and statistically insignificant to negative, economically small, and statistically insignificant. There is consensus in the academic literature that, on average, bidding shareholders do not experience significant, positive returns at the time of the merger announcement. This leads to two questions, one related to policy and the other technical.

The policy question. If, on average, bidding shareholders do not experience significant, positive returns at the time of the merger announcement, *is it possible to identify economic and financial characteristics of a subset of bidders whose shareholders have experienced significant positive returns from mergers?* What are the characteristics of the merger strategies of such acquirers? What are the characteristics of their bids? What can we learn from the postmerger activities of such acquirers? This book focuses on these interrelated questions.

The technical question. The academic literature has documented that, on average, bidding shareholders do not experience significant, positive returns at the time of the merger announcement. These findings are based on the analysis of the bidder's stock returns from a few days around the merger announcement. Some might argue that a few days around the merger announcement might not provide market participants with enough time or information to accurately assess the wealth consequence of the merger for the bidder's shareholders. After all, mergers and takeovers involving large bidders and targets are extremely complex transactions with elaborate financial, regulatory, and human resource implications. There are two counters to this line of reasoning, one conceptual and the other technical.

First, while mergers are complex transactions, other transactions, whose wealth implications have been analyzed and accepted with less controversy, are also complex. The following is a partial list of such transactions: dividend initiation/increase/decrease, share repurchase, equity offering and other capital structure changes, unexpected increases/decreases in R&D and capital expenditures, joint ventures, top management and governance changes. More important, for the very same merger transactions in question, there is wide consensus regarding the wealth impact on target shareholders.

Second, instead of just considering a few days around the merger announcement, one could consider the stock market returns from the merger announcement through one or two years postannouncement. Presumably during this one- or two-year postannouncement, market participants would have enough time and information to fully incorporate the wealth consequence of the merger on the bidder's share price. However, evidence in Kothari and Warner (1997) and Barber and Lyon (1997) suggests that stock return–based performance measures for a one- or two-year period are quite noisy and perhaps misspecified.

An alternative to stock market evidence is to examine accounting or other performance measures following completed transactions. Several studies have drawn very different conclusions about whether takeovers on average increase or decrease value; for example, see Healy, Palepu, and Ruback (1992), Kaplan and Weisbach (1991), Bhagat, Shleifer, and Vishny (1990). Although such studies are quite informative, they usually do not quantify the total discounted value of takeovers. More important, these studies are potentially subject to problems of noise and benchmark error analogous to those of stock market-based studies.

As noted, this book addresses the following question: *Is it possible to identify economic and financial characteristics of a subset of bidders whose shareholders have experienced significant positive returns from mergers?* Instead of considering the *average* wealth and value effects of mergers, this book focuses on a small sample of mergers where the bidding shareholders fared relatively well.

Sample Selection

A sample of all proposed mergers of U.S. targets between January 1990 and March 2002 was compiled. To focus our attention on recent mergers involving large publicly held acquirers and targets, we restricted our sample using the following criteria:

- A transaction value of at least $400 million
- The merger has been completed
- Both the target and bidder were publicly held at the time of merger announcement
- The merger was announced between January 1990 and March 2002

The above sample selection criteria yielded 906 merger transactions; the 100 largest of these are noted in Table 3.

Market Response around Merger Announcements

Table 1 provides the summary statistics for the transaction value, target valuation, premia paid, and acquirer stock returns (adjusted for market and size) from five trading days before through five trading days after the announcement of 906 takeover announcements in the United States between January 1990 and March 2002. Both the mean and median are -1 percent (and statistically significant); this result is consistent with the literature: Acquirers, in general, experience a small negative return at the time of a takeover announcement.

Market Response and Performance Postmerger

Table 1 also provides the summary statistics for the transaction value, target valuation, premia paid, and acquirer stock returns (adjusted for market and size) from five trading days before through five hundred trading days after (or June 30, 2002; whichever comes first) the announcement of 906 takeover announcements in the United States during January 1990–March 2002. Acquirer buy-and-hold returns (adjusted for market and size) from five trading days before through five hundred trading days are about -10 percent (and statistically significant).

Selection of Sample Where Bidders Fared Relatively Well

From the above sample of takeovers we selected those takeovers in which

- acquirer stock returns (adjusted for market and size) from five trading days before through five trading days after the announcement of the takeover were at least 4 percent
- acquirer buy-and-hold stock returns (adjusted for market and size) from five trading days before through (up to) five hundred trading days after the announcement of the

takeover were at least 30 percent. For bids made during 2000 and 2001 we consider returns through December 31, 2001.

The resulting sample of forty-four takeovers in which the bidders fared relatively well is noted in Table 2. Notice that this sample of forty-four bidders that fared relatively well includes bidders like Lucent, WorldCom, and Tyco. These three companies have performed rather poorly during the past year or two. These three bidders are in our sample of bidders that fared relatively well because the criterion for inclusion in this sample is the performance during the (approximate) two-year period subsequent to the bid. Lucent's bid was made on July 17, 1997, WorldCom's bid was made on September 8, 1997, and Tyco's on June 28, 2000. It would not be appropriate to impute the stock price performance of a company to an acquisition it had made several years in the past. The recent poor performance of these three bidders can only partially be attributed to their acquisition strategy.

Conclusion

A vast empirical literature in finance has documented that target shareholders experience large and statistically significant positive returns. In contrast, bidder shareholders experience a small negative or a small positive, but generally statistically insignificant, return. If, on average, bidding shareholders do not experience significant, positive returns at the time of the merger announcement, is it possible to identify economic and financial characteristics of a subset of bidders whose shareholders have experienced significant positive returns from mergers? This appendix has constructed such a sample of bidders, and the earlier chapters in the book focus on the characteristics of the merger strategies and postmerger activities of such acquirers.

Bibliography

Barber, B., J. Lyon, 1997. "Detecting Long-run Abnormal Stock Returns: The Empirical Power and Specification of Test Statistics." *Journal of Financial Economics* 43, 341–72.

Bhagat, S., M. Dong, D. Hirshleifer, and R. Noah, 2003. "Do Takeovers Create Value?" Working paper, University of Colorado.

Bhagat, S., A. Shleifer, and R. Vishny, 1990. Hostile Takeovers in the 1980's: The Return to Corporate Specialization. *Brookings Papers on Economic Activity*, 1–72.

Healy, P. M., K. G. Palepu, and R. S. Ruback, 1992. "Does Corporate Performance Improve after Mergers?" *Journal of Financial Economics* 31, 135–75.

Kaplan, S., and M. Weisbach, 1991. "The Success of Acquisitions: Evidence from Divestitures." *Journal of Finance* 47, 107–38.

Kothari, S. P., and J. Warner, 1997. "Measuring Long-horizon Security Price Performance." *Journal of Financial Economics* 43, 301–39.

TABLE I. Transaction value, target valuation, premia paid, and acquirer stock returns around the announcement of 906 takeover announcements in the U.S. during January 1990–March 2002

	5TH PERCENTILE	25TH PERCENTILE	MEDIAN	MEAN	75TH PERCENTILE	95TH PERCENTILE	SAMPLE SIZE	PERCENT POSITIVE
Value of transaction ($ mil)	427	621	1,201	3,658	2,820	12,415	906	
Value sales	.6	1.3	2.3	10.7	5.1	37.3	906	
Value cash flow	4.5	8.1	11.5	45.0	18.7	86.9	859	
Premium (%) 1 week prior to announcement date	0	16.8	32.1	38.1	51.8	95.7	906	
Premium (%) 4 weeks prior to announcement date	0	19.6	39.9	45.9	62.4	108.4	905	
Market price book value	1.3	2.1	3.2	8.0	5.7	20.4	866	
Acquirer stock returns (%) from 5 days before through 5 days after announcement	-19.7	-7.2	-1.4	-1.3	5.0	17.2	749	44
Acquirer stock returns (%) (adjusted for market and size) from 5 days before through 5 days after announcement	-19.4	-8.0	-1.6	-2.0	4.1	15.4	749	42
Acquirer stock returns (%) from 5 days before through 500 days after announcement	-120.3	-13.4	17.6	9.4	45.5	87.4	749	69
Acquirer stock returns (%) (adjusted for market and size) from 5 days before through 500 days after announcement	-137.9	-30.2	2.9	-6.7	28.0	72.7	749	53
Acquirer buy-and-hold stock returns (%) (adjusted for market and size) from 5 days before through 500 days after announcement	-85.6	-39.1	-9.1	-5.8	18.8	74.6	749	42

TABLE 2. Transaction value, target valuation, premia paid, and acquirer stock returns around the announcement of 906 takeover announcements in the U.S. during January 1990–March 2002 in which the acquirers fared well

Date Announced	Target Name	Acquirer Name	Value of Transaction ($mil)	Value/Sales	Value/Cash Flow	Premium 1 Week prior to Announcement Date	Premium 4 Weeks Prior to Ann. Date	Market/Book Value	Acquirer Stock Returns (%) from 5 Days before through 5 Days after Announcement	Acquirer Stock Returns (%) (Adjusted for Market and Size) from 5 Days before through 5 Days after Announcement	Acquirer Stock Returns (%) from 5 Days before through 500 Days after Announcement	Acquirer Stock Returns (%) (Adjusted for Market and Size) from 5 Days before through 500 Days after Announcement	Acquirer Buy-and-Hold Stock Returns (%) (Adjusted for Market and Size) from 5 Days before through 500 Days after Announcement
01/31/1991	Tonka Corp	Hasbro Inc	540	.687	5.233	37.93	53.85	.4	18	10	113	177	77
07/15/1991	Manufacturers HanoverCorp	Chemical Banking Corp	2044	.276	nm	-21.22	-23.99	.7	22	20	86	108	60
08/19/1993	Fisher-Price Inc	Mattel Inc	1145	1.617	10.816	35.42	43.6	3.8	12	9	74	96	48
05/30/1995	FirstFed Michigan Corp	Charter One Finl, Cleveland, OH	570	1.162	nm	14.78	23.11	1.2	9	8	82	114	31
08/28/1995	Chase Manhattan Corp	Chemical Banking Corp, NY	10440	0.974	41.759	7.46	5.45	1.4	22	20	86	120	31
02/13/1996	Citicasters Inc	Jacor Communications Inc	768	5.627	14.998	15.69	28.26	3.7	10	9	119	179	84
02/16/1996	Circle K Corp	Tosco Corp	983	.276	6.199	42.47	68.82	2.6	10	10	106	157	58
04/22/1996	StrataCom Inc	Cisco Systems Inc	4834	13.350	45.670	59.72	79.69	16.5	13	10	102	132	42
04/29/1996	Paul Revere Corp (Textron Inc)	Provident Cos	1171	0.751	7.289	5.58	8.9	.9	15	15	112	187	54

Date Announced	Target Name	Acquirer Name	Value of Transaction ($mil)	Value/Sales	Value/Cash Flow	Premium 1 Week prior to Announcement Date	Premium 4 Weeks Prior to Ann. Date	Market/Book Value	Acquirer Stock Returns (%) from 5 Days before through 5 Days after Announcement	Acquirer Stock Returns (%) (Adjusted for Market and Size) from 5 Days before through 5 Days after Announcement	Acquirer Stock Returns (%) from 5 Days before through 500 Days after Announcement	Acquirer Stock Returns (%) (Adjusted for Market and Size) from 5 Days before through 500 Days after Announcement	Acquirer Buy-and-Hold Stock Returns (%) (Adjusted for Market and Size) from 5 Days before through 500 Days after Announcement
04/30/1996	UUNet Technologies Inc	MFS Communications Inc Co	2061	16.830	nm	39.91	125.91	24.2	11	12	55	59	40
05/01/1996	Uniroyal Chemical (Avery Inc)	Crompton & Knowles Corp	1463	1.306	7.031	44.58	55.84		17	17	79	101	38
06/11/1997	Pacific Greystone Corp	Lennar Corp	459	2.757	23.450	83.3	98.45	9.1	20	18	106	125	78
07/17/1997	Octel Communications Corp	Lucent Technologies Inc	1825	2.936	14.581	37.4	41.31	4.0	11	8	156	284	109
09/08/1997	CompuServe Inc (H&R Block)	World Com Inc	1186	1.414	14.374	2.91	8.36	1.8	14	12	109	151	65
02/16/1998	Coherent Communications	SysTellabs Inc	664	9.014	30.160	43.23	81.37	13.5	10	8	133	150	91
03/01/1999	NeXstar Pharmaceuticals Inc	Gilead Sciences Inc	842	7.417	207.09	129.01	169.9	9.9	32	29	132	79	107
06/11/1999	Dynegy Inc	Illinova Corp	2852	.204	11.793	-6.42	-8.61	2.4	12	10	158	28	2136
06/23/1999	Omnipoint Corp	VoiceStream Wireless Corp	4816	23.141	nm	79.08	82.89		20	14	200	305	195

Date	Target	Acquirer											
07/19/1999	Vistana Inc	Starwood Hotels & Resorts	406	1.491	7.759	14.23	32.59	2.5	1	10	49	34	61
08/11/1999	Reynolds Metals Co	Alcoa Inc	6077	1.221	9.236	20.92	16.09	2.2	8	7	43	26	44
08/27/1999	Xomed Surgical Products Inc	Medtronic Inc	816	8.297	53.527	38.11	44.53	6.9	7	4	39	24	46
09/20/1999	Aerial Communications Inc	VoiceStream Wireless Corp	2478	12.836	nm	36.5	70.06	455.5	20	14	110	75	110
02/17/2000	US Home Corp	Lennar Corp	1501	.861	8.383	42.57	33.03	.9	20	18	128	183	52
03/14/2000	Cordant Technologies Inc	Alcoa Inc	2778	1.105	6.339	91.6	72.73	2.6	8	7	29	10	52
04/03/2000	Union Pacific Resources Group	Anadarko Petroleum Corp	7250	4.427	8.590	44.43	74.94	4.9	4	8	72	67	102
04/06/2000	Arvin Industries Inc	Meritor Automotive Inc	589	.196	2.505	5.06	22.22	1.1	0	10	60	37	64
04/10/2000	First Security Corp, Utah	Wells Fargo & Co, CA	2810	1.327	5.817	16.98	22.7	1.6	-3	7	18	11	44
05/17/2000	Keystone Finl, Harrisburg, PA	M&T Bank Corp, Buffalo, NY	1028	1.719	7.465	41.56	35.43	1.8	4	6	63	77	81
06/25/2000	Nabisco Holdings Corp (Nabisco)	Philip Morris Cos Inc	19275	2.272	13.837	5.26	17.96	3.7	6	6	77	94	97
06/28/2000	Mallinckrodt Inc	Tyco International Ltd	4393	1.668	8.251	74.06	63.16	3.1	8	9	41	37	65
07/27/2000	AXENT Technologies Inc	Symantec Corp	988	7.636	89.015	41.53	27.38	5.5	23	26	82	40	110
08/25/2000	Getthere.Com Inc	Sabre Holdings Corp	981	49.552	nm	97.22	63.22	4.0	22	18	66	48	87
10/26/2000	Keebler Foods Co	Kellogg Co	4652	1.725	10.792	20	8.04	7.5	13	6	36	36	49
11/03/2000	Fairfield Communities Inc	Cendant Corp	805	1.438	7.164	28	51.48	2.2	20	20	83	97	101

TABLE 2, continued

Date Announced	Target Name	Acquirer Name	Value of Transaction ($mil)	Value/Sales	Value/Cash Flow	Premium 1 Week prior to Announcement Date	Premium 4 Weeks Prior to Ann. Date	Market/Book Value	Acquirer Stock Returns (%) from 5 Days before through 5 Days after Announcement	Acquirer Stock Returns (%) (Adjusted for Market and Size) from 5 Days before through 5 Days after Announcement	Acquirer Stock Returns (%) from 5 Days before through 500 Days after Announcement	Acquirer Stock Returns (%) (Adjusted for Market and Size) from 5 Days before through 500 Days after Announcement	Acquirer Buy-and-Hold Stock Returns (%) (Adjusted for Market and Size) from 5 Days before through 500 Days after Announcement
11/09/2000	Benjamin-Moore and Co	Berkshire Hathaway Inc	1016	1.243	6.904	82.27	89.1	3.0	1	6	20	17	41
12/05/2000	Century South Banks Inc, GA	BB&T Corp, Winston-Salem, NC	427	3.027	14.265	44.97	64.3	2.7	10	7	20	19	33
12/18/2000	Morgan Keegan Inc	Regions Financial Corp	774	1.482	4.550	48.97	39.81	2.9	9	14	23	23	40
12/21/2000	Litton Industries Inc	Northrop Grumman Corp	5158	.973	8.329	32.23	33.47	2.4	12	11	30	28	46
12/21/2000	Great Plains Software Inc	Microsoft Corp	940	4.230	37.446	-19.82	6.47	3.1	2	5	26	16	41
01/30/2001	Wisconsin Central Transport	Canadian National Railway Co	1199	3.223		8.46	13.98	1.7	19	16	46	52	61
05/24/2001	Picture Tel Corp	Polycom Inc	412	1.795	nm	43.7	107.2	19.9	32	28	62	45	65
05/30/2001	MiniMed Inc	Medtronic Inc	3304	10.524	59.864	13.74	12.41	7.2	2	5	18	17	30
07/16/2001	Packard BioScience Co	Perkin Elmer Inc	623	3.325	24.530	2.21	46.41	4.4	19	19	38	40	41
08/22/2001	Arnold Roadway Industries Inc	Express Inc	554	1.216	6.200	7.67	11.71	1.9	9	10	37	38	35

TABLE 3: 100 Largest completed merger transactions involving U.S. targets during January 1990–March 2002

Date Announced	Target Name	Acquirer Name	% Shares of Acq.	Value of Transaction ($mil)	Value/Sales	Value/Cash Flow	Premium 1	Premium 4	Offering Price/Book Value
01/10/2000	Time Warner	America Online Inc	100.00	164746.461	6.027	15.173	55.81	70.19	14.7
11/04/1999	Warner-Lambert Co	Pfizer Inc	100.00	89167.72	6.897	30.278	29.68	40.82	18.5
12/01/1998	Mobil Corp	Exxon Corp	100.00	78945.79	1.253	10.962	34.71	16.66	4.2
04/06/1998	Citicorp	Travelers Group Inc	100.00	72558.18	2.043	9.833	10.4	18.97	3.5
04/13/1998	BankAmerica Corp	NationsBank Corp, Charlotte NC	100.00	61633.403	2.549	34.808	-.29	2.82	3.1
01/18/1999	AirTouch Communications Inc	Vodafone Group PLC	100.00	60286.874	12.915		50.17	71.45	7.2
06/14/1999	US WEST Inc	Qwest Commun Int Inc	100.00	56307.028	4.486	10.632	50.11	49.77	45.1
07/28/1998	GTE Corp	Bell Atlantic Corp	100.00	53414.579	2.185	6.106	-2.72	-4.94	6.8
04/22/1999	MediaOne Group Inc	AT&T Corp	100.00	49278.866	17.099	52.258	2.4	.88	3.5
08/11/1998	Amoco Corp	British Petroleum Co PLC	100.00	48174.085	1.407	8.203	25.27	22.03	3.1
10/16/2000	Texaco Inc	Chevron Corp	100.00	42872.30	.925	8.240	22.55	17.51	2.8
10/01/1997	MCI Communications Corp	WorldCom Inc	100.00	41906.90	2.745	14.756	100.99	94.29	3.7
07/10/2000	SDL Inc	JDS Uniphase Corp	100.00	41143.566	220.019	914.301	68.6	106.31	75.1
05/07/1998	Chrysler Corp	Daimler-Benz AG	100.00	40466.477	.654	4.893	54.25	45.73	3.3
09/07/1999	CBS Corp	Viacom Inc	100.00	39434.163	5.784	31.879	4.03	8.5	4.7
09/13/2000	JP Morgan & Co Inc	Chase Manhattan Corp, NY	100.00	33554.579	1.709	7.410	21.45	32.42	2.8
09/06/2000	Associates First Capital Corp	Citigroup Inc	100.00	30957.499	2.357	4.784	52.82	45.58	3.0
04/13/1998	First Chicago NBD Corp	BANC ONE Corp, Columbus, OH	100.00	29616.038	2.879	nm	8.58	20.34	3.7
07/24/2000	VoiceStream Wireless Corp	Deutsche Telekom AG	100.00	29404.372	12.263	107.605	-19.74	-19.61	3.0
04/01/2000	ARCO	BP Amoco PLC	100.00	27223.949	2.519		29.93	54.35	3.5
12/20/1999	Pharmacia & Upjohn Inc	Monsanto Co	100.00	26485.957	3.700		-6.45	-14.33	4.9
09/04/2001	Compaq Computer Corp	Hewlett-Packard Co	100.00	25263.447	.625	7.688	10.21	-2	2.1

TABLE 3 continued

Date Announced	Target Name	Acquirer Name	% Shares of Acq.	Value of Transaction ($mil)	Value/Sales	Value/Cash Flow	Premium 1	Premium 4	Offering Price/Book Value
05/02/2000	Bestfoods	Unilever PLC	100.00	25065.208	2.892	15.530	35.66	53.28	31.7
04/03/2001	American General Corp	American International Group	100.00	23398.157	2.115		17.92	-41.54	3.0
10/04/1999	AMFM Inc	Clear Channel Communications	100.00	23111.609	13.195	129.341	40.73	52.63	3.1
01/13/1999	Ascend Communications Inc	Lucent Technologies Inc	100.00	21422.965	16.538	55.315	27.49	196.07	14.6
04/22/1996	NYNEX Corp	Bell Atlantic Corp	100.00	21345.495	1.604	4.585	-.44	-5.68	3.2
03/07/2000	Network Solutions Inc	VeriSign Inc	100.00	21101.386	95.568	365.076	64.99	111.53	201.9
10/04/2000	US Bancorp, Minneapolis, MN	Firstar Corp, Milwaukee, WI	100.00	21084.873	2.284	13.837	32.84	27.94	2.7
06/25/2000	Nabisco Holdings Corp (Nabisco)	Philip Morris Cos Inc	100.00	19274.547	2.272	12.593	5.26	17.96	3.7
07/31/1995	Capital Cities/ABC Inc	Walt Disney Co	100.00	18836.74	2.815	39.732	25.19	15.18	4.1
03/29/2000	Seagate Technology Inc	Veritas Software Corp	100.00	18515.197	2.733	11.908	13.45	51.87	5.5
08/20/1998	SunAmerica Inc	American International Group	100.00	18116.984	8.553	4.300	35.4	32.9	5.3
07/12/2000	PaineWebber Group Inc	UBS AG	100.00	16542.565	2.209	4.154	64.02	53.52	3.8
04/01/1996	Pacific Telesis Group	SBC Communications Inc	100.00	16490.00	1.818	11.726	36.24	33.87	7.2
01/18/2000	Coastal Corp	El Paso Energy Corp	100.00	16006.384	1.953	11.075	33.81	36.57	2.5
03/14/1999	BankBoston Corp, Boston, MA	Fleet Financial Group Inc, MA	100.00	15925.201	2.082		25.45	48	3.2
08/16/1993	McCaw Cellular Commun Inc	American Telephone & Telegraph	89.45	15651.70	8.915		10.86	10.58	88.1
06/07/1999	Honeywell Inc	AlliedSignal Inc	100.00	15601.167	1.838	11.979	15.68	7.91	5.0
01/17/2000	E-Tek Dynamics Inc	JDS Uniphase Corp	100.00	15393.528	76.943	238.815	59.7	117.94	42.2
12/04/2000	Quaker Oats Co	PepsiCo Inc	100.00	14391.716	2.882	15.987	22.21	28.24	41.2
10/20/1997	ITT Corp	Starwood Hotels & Resorts	100.00	13748.211	2.085	14.130	98.25	95.4	3.2
08/26/1996	MFS Communications Co Inc	WorldCom Inc	100.00	13595.65	18.351	nm	59.96	86.96	18.3
12/17/1996	McDonnell Douglas Corp	Boeing Co	100.00	13359.00	.991	nm	22.71	20.08	4.5
04/16/2001	Wachovia Corp, Winston-Salem, NC	First Union Corp, Charlotte, NC	100.00	13132.151	1.772	8.379	8.3	4.66	2.0
12/07/1998	PacifiCorp	Scottish Power PLC	100.00	12599.626	1.691	10.881	37.95	35.71	1.9
08/03/1998	American Stores Co	Albertson's Inc	100.00	11864.608	.616	9.467	27.7	26	3.5

Date	Acquirer	Target							
08/08/2000	GPU Inc	FirstEnergy Corp	100.00	11826.922	2.252	6.831	36.77	29.49	1.4
08/04/1999	Union Carbide Corp	Dow Chemical Co	100.00	11691.51	2.066	10.256	37.35	32.92	3.6
05/27/1997	HFS Inc	CUC International Inc	100.00	11342.898	11.094	27.402	2.99	5.23	3.8
07/17/2000	Fort James Corp	Georgia-Pacific Corp	100.00	11198.472	1.629	8.849	58.16	56.91	7.3
03/27/2001	ALZA Corp	Johnson & Johnson	100.00	11070.277	11.199	32.125	25.26	6.43	6.4
06/25/2000	Nabisco Group Holdings Corp	RJ Reynolds Tobacco Holdings	100.00	11065.463	1.305	7.984	19.57	41.59	3.1
09/15/1999	General Instrument Corp	Motorola Inc	100.00	10935.528	5.138	32.091	5.45	11.63	4.9
02/18/1999	TransAmerica Corp	Aegon NV	100.00	10790.68	1.679	4.744	41.4	37.59	1.9
11/23/1998	AMP Inc	Tyco International Ltd	100.00	10735.623	1.906	9.811	11.16	18.24	3.7
04/30/1999	Mercantile Bancorp, St. Louis, MO	Firstar Corp, Milwaukee, WI	100.00	10640.485	3.627	16.566	-64.75	-64.71	3.4
02/05/1997	Morgan Stanley Group Inc	Dean Witter Discover & Co	100.00	10573.01	.804	1.161	12.8	13.81	1.9
01/15/2001	Ralston Purina Co	Nestle SA	100.00	10479.411	3.788	16.436	38.86	30.41	18.3
08/28/1995	Chase Manhattan Corp	Chemical Banking Corp, NY	100.00	10439.78	.974	41.759	7.46	5.45	1.4
03/17/1999	Frontier Corp	Global Crossing Ltd	100.00	10062.55	3.880	18.525	27.38	41.58	8.4
08/30/1996	Boatmen's Bancshares, St Louis	NationsBank Corp, Charlotte, NC	100.00	9667.10	3.137	11.331	48.36	48.36	2.7
04/25/2000	Champion International Corp	International Paper Co	100.00	9640.103	1.798	10.740	48.33	21.21	2.3
09/09/1993	Paramount Communications	Viacom Inc (Natl Amusements)	100.00	9600.00	2.305	19.810	88.55	98.15	3.2
08/02/1994	American Cyanamid Co	American Home Products Corp	99.99	9560.90	2.003		64.23	80.76	5.2
02/04/2001	Tosco Corp	Phillips Petroleum Co Inc	100.00	9388.283	.382	6.724	38.82	45.04	2.6
03/13/2001	CIT Group Inc	Tyco International Ltd	100.00	9340.533	1.516	1.902	47.63	46.83	1.5
06/15/1998	Bay Networks Inc	Northern Telecom Ltd (BCE Inc)	100.00	9268.604	3.967	204.096	18.49	44.88	5.6
03/13/2000	Times Mirror Co	Tribune Co	83.73	9230.656	3.639	17.309	84.24	68.89	
08/18/2000	R&B Falcon Corp	Transocean Sedco Forex Inc	100.00	9091.488	10.475	42.905	26.44	36.54	5.0
10/04/1999	TV Guide (Tele-Communications)	Gemstar International Group	100.00	9084.802	9.511	47.858	40.49	95.44	5.5
03/05/1999	Browning-Ferris Industries Inc	Allied Waste Industries Inc	100.00	9053.729	2.034	7.817	42.86	46.06	5.2
04/01/1996	US Healthcare Inc	Aetna Life & Casualty Co	100.00	8939.04	2.380	15.718	21.28	18.75	7.9
03/20/1997	US Bancorp, Portland, OR	First Bank Sys, Minneapolis, MN	100.00	8928.917	2.953	11.913	79.37	83.9	3.4
09/24/1997	Salomon Inc	Travelers Group Inc	100.00	8852.113	1.003	1.401	24.08	34.6	1.9
01/08/1996	Loral Corp	Lockheed Martin Corp	100.00	8762.38	1.418	9.310	7.42	8.19	3.4
02/28/2000	Columbia Energy Group	NiSource Inc	100.00	8500.536	2.665	9.688	21.13	11.69	2.9
05/27/1999	Outdoor Systems Inc	Infinity Broadcasting Corp	100.00	8466.746	12.566	26.509	14.04	26.83	8.1
09/05/2000	Niagara Mohawk Holdings Inc	National Grid Group PLC	100.00	8047.669	1.876	6.769	49.02	35.71	1.1
08/22/1999	Florida Progress Corp	Carolina Power & Light Co	100.00	7984.213	2.143	7.748	26.69	29.34	2.7
03/13/2000	Aspect Development Inc	i2 Technologies Inc	100.00	7974.212	83.811	1056.327	24.69	109.19	68.6

TABLE 3 continued

Date Announced	Target Name	Acquirer Name	% Shares of Acq.	Value of Transaction ($mil)	Value/Sales	Value/Cash Flow	Premium 1	Premium 4	Offering Price/Book Value
01/07/1994	Blockbuster Entertainment Corp	Viacom Inc (Natl Amusements)	100.00	7971.07	3.579	8.794	17.12	26.31	3.8
12/02/1990	NCR Corp	American Telephone & Telegraph	100.00	7893.40	1.235	8.112	134.37	108.45	4.1
11/13/2000	Willamette Industries Inc	Weyerhaeuser Co	100.00	7857.313	1.764	10.429	57.17	106.03	2.4
02/26/1998	Dresser Industries Inc	Halliburton Co	100.00	7783.242	1.044	9.099	15.03	18.32	4.5
05/10/1999	Republic New York Corp, NY	HSBC Holdings PLC	100.00	7702.864	2.187	17.161	19.76	30.03	2.9
11/25/1996	PanEnergy Corp	Duke Power Co	100.00	7666.829	1.217	7.571	22.7	30.29	3.3
09/24/1990	MCA Inc	Matsushita Electric Industrial	100.00	7406.00	1.909	4.612	78.38	54.39	2.5
09/23/1999	Unicom Corp	PECO Energy Co	100.00	7386.18	1.079	3.041	-12.8	-13.91	1.4
12/13/1999	USWeb/CKS	Whitman-Hart Inc	100.00	7280.437	18.354	nm	42.26	80.1	10.2
02/28/1995	Marion Merrell Dow Inc	Hoechst AG	100.00	7264.57	2.374	10.393	14.44	11.35	3.4
04/03/2000	Union Pacific Resources Group	Anadarko Petroleum Corp	100.00	7250.069	4.427	8.590	44.43	74.94	4.9
09/12/1996	Duracell International Inc	Gillette Co	100.00	7231.94	3.159	13.341	29.75	30.11	5.0
07/01/1998	Firstar Corp, Milwaukee, WI	Star Banc Corp, Cincinnati, OH	100.00	7217.594	3.720	14.201	44.1	33.69	4.0
07/28/2000	Alteon Websystems Inc	Nortel Networks Corp	100.00	7056.886	106.923	nm	.01	43.68	23.6
12/01/1997	First of Amer Bk, Kalamazoo, MI	National City, Cleveland, OH	100.00	7052.65	3.365	13.045	40.22	43.04	3.8
08/09/2000	Software.com Inc	Phone.com Inc	100.00	7047.321	92.122	nm	27.8	2.21	36.5
02/23/2001	Spieker Properties Inc	Equity Office Properties Trust	100.00	7020.514	8.177	11.177	10.62	12.1	2.8
10/02/2000	Summit Bancorp, Princeton, NJ	FleetBoston Financial Corp, MA	100.00	7011.635	2.345	9.166	41.13	48.71	2.4
06/21/2000	Burr-Brown Corp	Texas Instruments Inc	100.00	6956.013	23.867	88.416	82.16	109.14	19.4

Value of Transaction ($ mil): Total value of consideration paid by the acquirer, excluding fees and expenses. The dollar value includes the amount paid for all common stock, common stock equivalents, preferred stock, debt, options, assets, warrants, and stake purchases made within six months of the announcement date of the transaction. Liabilities assumed are included in the value if they are publicly disclosed. If a portion of the consideration paid by the acquirer is common stock, the stock is valued using the closing price on the last full trading day prior to the announcement of the terms of the stock swap. If the exchange ratio of shares offered changes, the stock is valued based on its closing price on the last full trading date prior to the date of the exchange ratio change.

Ratio of Value to Cash Flow: Transaction value divided by target cash flow for the 12 months ending on the date of the most current financial information prior to the announcement of the transac-

tion. The result is divided by the percentage of the company acquired in the deal.

Value-to-Sales Ratio: Transaction value divided by the target's net sales for the past 12 months ending on the date of the most current financial information prior to the announcement of the transaction. The result is divided by the percentage of the company acquired in the deal.

Premium 1 Week Prior to Announcement Date: Premium of offer price to target trading price 1 week prior to the original announcement date.

Premium 4 Weeks Prior to Announcement Date: Premium of offer price to target trading price 4 weeks prior to the original announcement date.

Ratio of Price to Book Value, 4 Weeks Prior to Announcement Date: Target stock price 4 weeks prior to announcement date of the transaction divided by target book value as of the date of the most current financial information prior to the announcement of the transaction.